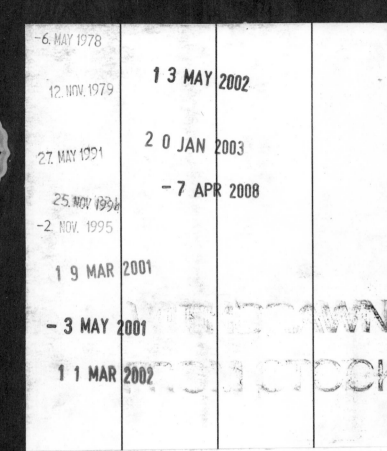

Japan is a world in miniature. From a thousand images I have selected those which give the most faithful visual expression to my own personal encounter with this country of infinite nuances. They will, I hope, evoke the rich dimensions of a land I saw in all seasons: its grand natural landscapes and those recreated for private contemplation in their gardens; their intimate features so fresh yet hauntingly familiar—for nature seems everywhere to imitate the art forms evolved by the Japanese over two thousand years.

Thus I have denied myself a preface, trusting that the photographs between these covers will speak to the uninitiated and even to the many in Japan itself who made my undertaking an enchantment through their willingness to share the beauty of their land and unique way of life.

To those many individuals and organizations who so readily offered their help, and indeed to all the people of Japan who combine the poetry of their heritage so effectively with their vitality of today . . . I dedicate this book with a quotation from a poem of the Kamakura era:

The sound of the bell of Gion-shoja echoes
The impermanence of all things . . .
like evening dreams in spring time
they are
but as the dust before the wind

ROLOFF BENY
Rome 1967

Cormorant-fishing, Gifu

Japan
IN COLOUR

Photographed by
ROLOFF BENY

Text by
ANTHONY THWAITE

Introduction by
HERBERT READ

96 plates in colour

THAMES AND HUDSON · LONDON

The lines of Dr. Daisetz Suzuki which Herbert Read quotes in his Introduction are taken from Zen and Japanese Culture *and are reproduced by kind permission of the publishers Routledge & Kegan Paul Ltd, London, and the Bollingen Foundation, New York.*

Anthony Thwaite has used in his text English versions of haiku *from* The Penguin Book of Japanese Verse *(ed. Geoffrey Bownas and Anthony Thwaite).*

The map of Japan on page 41 was drawn by Mrs. Hanni Bailey.

© HERBERT READ (INTRODUCTION) ANTHONY THWAITE (MAIN TEXT AND NOTES)
ROLOFF BENY (PHOTOGRAPHS) 1967
TEXT SET BY KEYSPOOLS LTD LANCASHIRE ENGLAND BY "MONOPHOTO" PROCESS
AND PRINTED BY DRUCKEREI WINTERTHUR AG WINTERTHUR SWITZERLAND
COLOUR PLATES PRODUCED BY TRINI AG FÜR TIEFDRUCKERZEUGNISSE BREMEN WEST GERMANY
BOOK BOUND BY KORNELIUS KASPERS DÜSSELDORF WEST GERMANY

THE PLATES

IMAGES OF A LANDSCAPE

GARDENS AND TEMPLES: THE GRAMMAR OF DESIGN

CUSTOM AND CEREMONY: THE GESTURES OF A PEOPLE

IMAGES OF PERMANENCE

日本

INTRODUCTION

'TO UNDERSTAND THE CULTURAL LIFE OF THE JAPANESE PEOPLE in all its different aspects', writes the best of its interpreters, Dr. Daisetz Suzuki, 'it is essential to delve into the secrets of Zen Buddhism. Without some knowledge of these the Japanese character is difficult to appreciate.' To some degree the same relationship exists between the cultural life of every nation and its traditional religion, but Zen Buddhism, which crossed from the mainland of China in the thirteenth century, became in Japan in a very special sense a religion of beauty.

In other cultures, the Greek for example, beauty has been associated with religion; even the Christian, often so distrustful of beauty in some of its sensuous manifestations, speaks of 'the beauty of holiness'. But neither Greek religion nor Christianity ever regarded the appreciation of beauty as an appropriate and even a necessary method of insight into the nature of reality. Most religions sooner or later begin to rely on conceptual modes of thought: they elaborate a *system* of belief, issue moral commands, sacrifice their original concreteness to metaphysical abstractions. This is precisely what Zen had strived to avoid. Its teaching is embodied in the *koan* or in the *mondo*, riddles often accompanied by a violent gesture. In a similar manner Christ embodied his teaching in simple parables. From the *koan* and the *mondo* it was but one step to the *haiku*, the typical form of Japanese poetry, said to have been invented by Bashō (1643–94), a Zen master. In Japan all the arts—painting, architecture, gardening, and the arts peculiar to Japan such as the tea ceremony and flower arrangement—are imbued with the spirit of Zen and derive their special aesthetic qualities from this fact.

For seven centuries Zen has moulded the Japanese way of life in all its more intimate aspects, and intimacy is the characteristic we must emphasise, for it distinguishes the art inspired by Zen from all other types of art. There are, of course, intimate arts in other cultures—the art of miniature painting in Islam, for example, the art of porcelain figures in the Rococo period in Europe, Renaissance jewellery, and many other arts in every part of the world. But these other arts are exquisite rather than intimate—intimacy, as practised by the Japanese artist, implies a particular relationship to Nature, shared by a poet such as Wordsworth, but not really characteristic of the visual arts in any countries other than China and Japan. Intimacy, in this sense, is a personal identification of the artist with the spirit of Nature, but not in the quietist sense typical of Western mysticism. To quote Suzuki again: 'It is not a sense of identity nor of tranquillity that Zen sees and loves in Nature. Nature is always in motion, never at a standstill; if Nature is to be loved, it must be caught while moving and in this way its aesthetic value must be appraised. To seek tranquillity is to kill nature, to stop its pulsation, and to embrace the dead corpse that is left behind. Advocates of tranquillity are worshippers of abstraction and death.'

Perhaps Bashō's famous *haiku*, the prototype of thousands of poems of this kind, illustrates Suzuki's meaning:

Furu ike ya!   *An old pond:*

Kawazu tobikomu   *A frog jumps in—*

Mizu no oto.   *Sound of water.*

A *haiku* presents a vision of natural objects, in significant association, and the infinite reverberations of this moment of vision in the mind of the observer. As Suzuki points out, the *haiku* does not express ideas, but puts forward images reflecting intuitions. 'As long as we are moving on the surface of consciousness, we can never get away from ratiocination; the old pond is understood as symbolising solitude and tranquillity, and a frog jumping into it and the sound thereof are taken for instruments whereby to set off and also to increase the general sense of eternal

8

quietness. But Bashō the poet is not living there as we are, he has passed through the outer crust of consciousness away down into its deepest recesses, into a realm of the unthinkable, into the Unconscious, which is even beyond the unconscious generally conceived by the psychologists. Bashō's old pond lies on the other side of eternity, where timeless time is. . . . No scale of consciousness can measure it. It is whence all things come, it is the source of this world of particulars, yet in itself it shows no particularisation.'

'This world of particulars'—this gives us the clue to Roloff Beny's approach to Japanese culture, to Japanese art and the Japanese landscape. It is a world of particulars (not of panoramas, of general views, of vast monuments) and it has to be seen with the eyes of a poet, with Bashō's eyes. Beny sees such things as old ponds, broken stones, the iris and the cherry blossom, shadows on walls and the texture of a moss garden all 'on the other side of eternity', as all the great Japanese artists have seen such particulars. It is quite astonishing to observe the way in which this camera-eye from the West can identify itself with the Zen vision of the realm of the unthinkable, the world of pure vision, free from all attempts at an intellectual interpretation of such things.

The camera is a mechanism, and one's first thought is that as such it is alien to the world of Zen; but the mechanism embodied in the camera is merely a spring that releases and imprints a moment of vision; that moment of vision is an extension of a human vision, the vision of an artist. In the hands of an artist the camera can penetrate to 'the timelessness of the Unconscious'; it can combine the two worlds of the sensual and the supersensual. It can register that moment of consciousness when the meaning of existence is revealed in a visual image. To quote another famous *haiku*, this one by Buson (1716–83):

> *Tsuri-gane ni*   *On the temple bell*
>
> *Tomarite nemuru*   *Perching, sleeps*
>
> *Kocho kana*   *The butterfly, oh!*

Since the camera is an extension of the poet's eye such an image, essentially visual, such a collocation of significant particulars, can be perfectly registered by it. Whatever interpretation we make of this *haiku* (and Suzuki devotes several pages to its significance) can also be made of a photograph that depicts a visual metaphor of the same kind. Roloff Beny is a poet in search of visual metaphors.

The significance of this *haiku* perhaps cannot be appreciated unless we consider the peculiar characteristics of the Japanese temple or shrine, so frequently illustrated in this book. It has little in common with the Western conception of a temple or a church, and any such unified complex as a Christian cathedral just does not exist in Japan, until we come to the modern age, when you find imitations of Western-style architecture, such as the Olympic stadium or the new Roman Catholic cathedral, in Tokyo. The temple is usually a barn-like wooden structure with open sides, approached through one or more *torii* or gateways and giving onto a setting of trees and rocks and raked paths. There will be one or more figures of the Buddha, placed in unlit niches, and there may be an altar for sacrifices and a few stools for the priests. The priests themselves have bare, modest dormitories to live in, without privacy or comfort, though the abbot will have a private room in which he receives visitors, and sometimes there are small rooms where the monks may retire to meditate. The temple bell will be hung on a detached framework, near the ground for ease of striking with a wooden mallet, and a place where a butterfly would naturally settle on it. Everywhere there are rocks and pine-trees, and perhaps the sound of running water. But nothing to intimidate the visitor— everything is on a natural scale, and in harmony with the living things that surround the temple. Yet if you look closer at the actual structure, at the adzed and morticed beams, then you will discover the secret beauty of the temple. Every detail is made with respect for the nature of the material (usually timber), and every measurement matches every other measurement in perfect harmony. Such harmony is achieved by using natural materials in their pristine state, combining them by methods which do not contradict their modes of growth, and by an instinctive and infallible sense of proportion. The temple does not rise defiantly against the laws of gravity, or strive to impress mankind by its magnitude: it strives not to offend against the laws of nature, to be a holy *place* rather than an artificial structure.

I must not give the impression that the Japanese scene consists entirely of such poetic images, or that the influence of Zen is everywhere evident in Japan. On the contrary, modern Japan is a highly competitive, rapidly developing industrial economy, and the whole country is scarred by hideous conurbations of factories, mines, foundries, petrol-stations, docks, housing-estates, indistinguishable from such developments in Europe or America. The Zen spirit has not penetrated modern Japanese industry (though there are some notable exceptions, such as the Idemitsu Oil Refinery at Tokuyama). The shrines and temples of Shinto and Zen are now artificial reservations in the midst of this turmoil, and if one visits them in the hope of finding an oasis of tranquillity, the same thought will have occurred to several hundred noisy tourists— tourism is one of the scourges of modern Japan, as of every highly developed industrial society. But there does come a moment, perhaps at sunrise or sunset, when a stillness descends on the scene, and then in that moment the poet feels, with Wordsworth—

> *Gleams like the flashing of a shield; the earth*
> *And common face of Nature spake to me*
> *Rememberable things; sometimes, 'tis true*
> *By chance collisions and quaint accidents . . .*

Wordsworth's 'chance collisions and quaint accidents' also describes the moment of enlightenment that Roloff Beny seeks with his camera. It is important to emphasise that this enlightenment is found, not in ascetic practices nor in a withdrawal from the world, but in 'our daily concrete particular experiences, such as eating, drinking, or business of all kind'. The camera is a perfect instrument for recording such concrete particular experiences, such chance collisions and quaint accidents.

Just as Buson would sometimes combine the words of his *haiku* with a visual image—for example, an outline of Mount Fuji followed by the words:

> *. . . alone*
>
> *Left unburied*
>
> *By young green leaves,*

so, the text and illustrations in this volume must be combined. Although the visual image, as captured by Beny, has the same function as the *haiku* or a painting by Sesshu or Sengai, or any work of art that gives significance to the minute particulars of our mysterious universe, it would be contrary to the Japanese spirit to rely on any one art, or to suppose that any one artist holds the key to the mystery. The Japanese artist is a modest pragmatist: that is why he never aspires to the monumental work of art, to the grandiose epic or metaphysical ode. The manner in which Anthony Thwaite's understanding text complements Beny's photographs in this respect is entirely in keeping with Japanese thought.

'If our real nature is creative like nature itself, wherever we may be, we see that all things are free like sporting fishes and circling kites.' That quotation from the *Saikontan*, a seventeenth-century anthology of significant texts, may fittingly conclude this Introduction, which has sought to demonstrate that the spirit who conceived this book was creative like nature itself, and for this reason, all that he has seen and recorded with his camera has a natural freedom.

HERBERT READ

JAPAN

THE MOST EXTRAORDINARY THING ABOUT JAPAN is that it is so very Japanese. Fuji seen in a red and black sunset at the end of some Tokyo suburban lane, small, clear, perfect, like a postage-stamp reproduction: the branch of a pine framing, with tortured elegance, a wall of cyclopean masonry: the litter of fallen cherry petals in a puddle: a grove of bamboo after a shower of rain. These natural snapshots abstracted from the memory are all true, all typical, and all sum up a received notion of Japan—a land where nature imitates art. The Japanese have been such loving delineators of the shapes and postures of their country that the traveller knows the place the moment he arrives, its patterns are printed on his retina as he steps ashore at Yokohama or lands at Haneda.

But Japan is not only a country of the eye. Its sensuousness—and nowhere is more sensuous—draws on all the faculties. To read Japanese poetry is to be aware of a succession of aural as well as visual impressions:

> *The cuckoo—*
> *Its call stretching*
> *Over the water.*

> *Scampering over saucers—*
> *The sound of a rat.*
> *Cold, cold.*

> *All its advertisements*
> *Given over to the wind—*
> *The windbell shop.*

The first is seventeenth-century, the second eighteenth-century, the last modern. All share not only a common verse form but a common sensibility. And not only in poetry. When I think of a distinguished modern Japanese novelist, Kawabata Yasunari, and his novel *Snow Country*, what comes back to me? Not the narrative, which I forget—Japanese novelists have never been strong on narrative—nor the characters, but a brief description of skis steaming in winter sunshine, of the sound of a steaming tea-kettle merging with the chime of a temple bell. And Kawabata is only one of many. Nagai Kafu, who died in 1959, was a novelist whose whole art lay in the impressionistic recording of the sights, sounds and smells of his native city, Tokyo; in his stories, the plaintive twang of a *samisen* carries the burden and resonance of plot or dialogue in a European novel.

This has something to do, perhaps, with that delicacy and refinement which some foreigners find themselves too gross to respond to in Japan; and which, also, they find difficult to square with what they have heard (or even, in war, experienced) of Japanese brutality. There are apparent paradoxes, certainly. Write a rapid list of the thoughts suggested by the word *Japan* and the paradoxes leap up from the page immediately: cherry blossom, little yellow men with rabbit teeth and glasses, Fuji, paper houses, earthquakes, Hiroshige, *geisha*, the Rape of Nanking, ships, cameras, transistors, Toyotas, *saké*, *Noh* plays, *Rashomon*, Hiroshima, the chrysanthemum and the sword. . . . What does one extrapolate from this, what makes sense, which is the *true* Japan?

As with many countries or cultures, perhaps it is best to begin with a few words: key words, which are untranslatable and yet which (perhaps for that reason) are extremely important to an understanding of that country or culture. One might begin with *kokushin*, which is usually given as 'national spirit' or 'national polity'. No people is more aware of its nationality than the Japanese. You can't be very long in Japan before you hear someone beginning a sentence with 'We Japanese . . .' It is not self-consciousness: it is national consciousness. 'What are your impressions of Japan?' someone asks (not by any means necessarily a journalist) five minutes after your arrival. Your answer is noted, but whatever it is it will confirm the Japanese-ness of Japan. They *know* that they are distinct from other races: the ignorant or the unsophisticated will simply take it for granted, the intellectual will have reasons, but both will be firm in their distinction. The years of Tokugawa, the years of deliberate and almost complete isolation from the world between 1639 and 1853, created an *us/them* dichotomy which it will take much more than another two hundred years to blend or patch up. In one sense these years behind a bamboo screen bred stagnation, in another they established an astonishingly single-minded purity of culture. Everything that had been absorbed in the previous centuries stewed or matured with a remote intensity: Buddhism, Confucianism, even Christianity (strange forms of Marianism sprang up among the tiny persecuted band of converts made by Francis Xavier in Nagasaki); weaving, metal-casting, silkworm culture, brewing, writing, poetry. . . . What Commodore Perry found was, in a way, a fossil society. But a fossil lacks life, and Tokugawa Japan had very much a self-absorbed, preoccupied life of its own. Here are the roots of modern, and continuing, Japan, in the hidden years when she grew towards *kokushin*.

Then, almost at random, a second word: *awaré*. 'Lacrimae rerum', perhaps, the eternal sadness of things, the fleeting beauty of nature and of life. This is deep within the spirit of Japanese poetry—in Uejima Onitsura (1661–1738), for example:

> *They bloom and then*
> *We look and then they*
> *Fall and then . . .*

Or, as a girl student of mine once wrote in an essay, of cherry blossom and its importance to the Japanese, 'We love the cherry blossoms because they are most beautiful in the moment of their death.' Yes, morbidity: very well. But it is a morbidity based on fact, not fancy. In a country which knows earthquake, fire, flood and typhoon as Japan does, the precariousness of existence is something you posit from the start. To sum it all up in the falling blossom, in the regular cycle of the seasons, is a kind of sublimation or externalisation—perhaps it could be explained in that sort of way. Hiroshima and Nagasaki were not, to the Japanese, disasters because the bombs destroyed flesh and blood on a hideous scale: 'All flesh is grass' might as easily be a line from a Japanese *haiku* as a line from the Bible, because the transience and momentariness of human life is the very stuff of their resignation, their stoicism, their *awaré*. The atomic disaster was the major shock to their sense of *kokushin*. The great Kanto earthquake of 1923, which largely destroyed Tokyo and Yokohama, killed many more people than the two 1945 bombs. But an earthquake is both a source of and, by extension, a product of *awaré*.

So *awaré* is nature in eternal decay. *Shibui* is a kind of beauty which may be associated with it—a kind of beauty characterised by simplicity, roughness, irregularity, subtlety. You can see it in nature: sometimes in an autumn leaf, which of itself has grown muted, patinated, dulled and brilliant at the same moment; sometimes when man has taken part and tutored a miniature tree, a *bonsai*, into a form surprising without being grotesque. And you can see it in art—in the inclination to leave something out in a poem, or in a Sesshu painting where one bold stroke among the vaguer hinted rest seems almost wrong and yet somehow right, or in a pot by the master Kawai Kanjiro, where the cup sags a little to the left or has a muted grey severity. In art, in the decorative arts, *shibui* may have something to do with poverty: I remember Kawai once saying that the Japanese have made a virtue of their poverty, allowing it to dictate the stringency of their methods. It is a style of life, or a style of living, which makes a man eschew ostentation and vulgarity.

This seems to be true of traditional products at least. Alongside a plastic kewpie doll you may find a beautifully simple and subtle tea-bowl: the owner will have criteria by which to judge the merits of the bowl, but the doll is outside his frame of reference. In the Nikkatsu arcade in Tokyo, a favourite haunt of tourists, there are flamboyant *kimono* on sale, voluminous affairs in black silk with red-eyed golden dragons; but no Japanese buy them, they are made for the tourist with his supposedly inflamed ideas of the gorgeous East: properly Japanese *kimono* and *yukata* are always restrained in design, and draw on a limited range of natural vegetable

16

colours. In the same way, there is no native domestic equivalent of those plaster or ceramic wall-ducks, Negro heads, or airedales at bay, though this is not to say that Japanese don't sometimes buy such things. And—to look at *shibui*, at Japanese aesthetic sense, another way—for all the almost frontier-town clutter of a suburban Tokyo street of shops, one has only to contrast this with the chain-store gloom of an American or British shopping-centre to feel that in Japan even the makeshift has a sense of style. Which is why the gold and glare of the buildings at Nikko are so very un-Japanese, however much the tourist literature urges you to go there or however often you hear repeated the old saw, 'Never say *kekko* (magnificent) until you've seen Nikko'. Indeed, I've sometimes wondered whether there isn't an implied sneer in that phrase; for what Japanese, confronted with a work of art, would prefer to comment *kekko* rather than *shibui*?

And Japan's apotheosising of poverty, for all the present heady talk of boom and progress, comes from a real source, a real poverty. Only about eighteen per cent of the country can be farmed. The small plots are intensively worked, the rice-paddies crowded in narrow valleys, the tea-bushes perched precariously on steep hill slopes. The country is not blessed with rich natural resources, either in agriculture or in minerals. Hard work, clever management, inventive power, a compact of accepted responsibilities and loyalties—all these have contributed to the post-war resurgence, keeping industrialists from Manchester to Cincinnati on the trot. But underneath is an unfriendly land, mountainous, unproductive, subject to violent natural hazards, overpopulated. It is not one of those Hesperidean places where you throw in a few seeds and watch them spring up, blossom and burgeon overnight. You have to nurture the seeds with your own dung, because animals take up too much valuable space. And no number of Toyotas zooming off the assembly lines is going to alter that.

In a country as naturally recalcitrant as Japan, brains and industry have to unite to win. But *brains* is not just a matter of technical know-how: knowledge and the cultivation of knowledge are respected for themselves, for their own sakes. Which brings me to a fourth

Japanese word: *bunka*. It has an unfortunate sound to a British or American ear, with 'History is bunk' hovering somewhere, and doubly unfortunate when one learns that it means, very broadly, 'culture'. Yet no Japanese reaches for his gun when he hears the word. To be a *bunka-jin*, an intellectual, is no slur, and the word carries such an aura that sometime after the war there came on the market a product with the trade-name *Bunka-nabé*, 'culture saucepan'.

Bunka, I suppose, begins with being able to read and write; and the statistics say that 99·8 per cent of the Japanese can read and write the *kanji* (Chinese ideograms) in normal use—about 1800 characters—as well as the *kana*, the syllabaries used for transliterating the large number of foreign words in Japanese. On a train or bus in Japan it is very rare to see anyone just sitting (or standing) and vacantly staring, as one frequently does in the West. Passengers may be reading newspapers, but many will be reading books, or such big-circulation cultural magazines as *Bungei-Shunju* or *Chuo-Kuron*, which have a staple of intellectual news and comment. Ordinary people are incredibly well-informed about what is going on in the cinema, the theatre, and in the latest novels; and, at a lower level, even more popular magazines present photographs of contemporary novelists and poets disporting themselves at home and in bars, in a way that only singers and entertainers expect in Europe and America. I remember, on my last visit to Japan, the distinguished novelist Mishima Yukio coming to visit me in my hotel, and by the time he left the word had got round, for as he reached the *genkan* to put on his shoes and go, a large number of the hotel staff had turned up to get a glimpse of the famous man and bow him farewell. The equivalent, in British terms, would be the popular mobbing of Kingsley Amis in South Kensington: an unlikely prospect.

For a population of about ninety-five million, there are 591 universities and colleges, with nearly 800,000 students enrolled. One can take a strict view and say that many of these are what we would call training-colleges, academies of art and music, and the like; but even after saying that, one has to acknowledge an astonishing efflorescence of 'higher education'. The struggle to get into the top universities (for example, the old Imperial universities, such as Tokyo,

Kyoto, and Tohoku at Sendai, and the big private foundations such as Keio and Waseda) is gruelling and fierce. Suicide after failure is not uncommon. Once inside, the student may perhaps be excused if the pace slackens a bit, but working conditions in Japanese universities are uncomfortably Spartan: two-hour lectures sitting on hard wooden benches in draughty halls are a test of endurance, and who can blame the weaker students for sneaking off into the warmth and darkness of a coffee-bar—often with a comfortingly intellectual or *bunka*-laden name, such as the Bar Rilke or the Bar Rimbaud.

Not that one should imagine these university students as dreamy fellows somnambulising through their academic years. Because of the smallness of the government grants, they usually have to find themselves part-time work, sometimes fairly congenially as tutors to high-school students attempting the entrance examinations, more often as waiters, porters and labourers. This *arbeit* (the German word is used) is not a casual business of picking up a bit of pocket money, as it often is in Britain and America, but a hard slog to earn the necessities; and students turn up at the university exhausted after working all night. Students are also the spearhead of political activism in the country, at both extremes of left and right. The all-Japan student union, *Zengakuren*, can quickly and efficiently turn on a demonstration or a strike, and *demo* and *sturaiko* are words that have entered the language. The strike or demonstration may be to do with an unpopular foreign visit (such as Eisenhower's famously aborted trip), or against some new Ministry of Education ruling, or—perhaps most typically—concerned with showing reactions to the latest move in the nuclear game. But fanaticism can be tempered with a gentle commonsense, a gentle irony, which is just as much a part of the Japanese spirit. One Friday in 1956 I turned up at the Komaba 'campus' of Tokyo University as usual, to give one of a series of lectures on Shakespeare. All my students appeared to be dutifully, note-takingly, there. The next day I read in the newspaper that on Friday there had been a nation-wide student strike organised by Zengakuren, in protest against the British nuclear tests at Christmas Island. I was puzzled, and when I saw my students again on Monday I asked a group of them why they had apparently defied their union to come to my lecture. One of them smiled a little roguishly and replied, 'Ah yes, sir, but Shakespeare did not drop an atomic bomb.'

This—which I suppose one can call 'sensitiveness', but it seems a clumsy and inaccurate word—is a basic trait of the Japanese. It expresses itself in exquisite private manners, in an almost embarrassing thoughtfulness and generosity. One is loaded with presents on the slightest pretext. Teachers are inundated with dolls, sets of spoons, sets of *saké* cups, ornaments of all sorts, and I remember in one case a very large fish, too large to accommodate in any but the biggest refrigerator; and all this simply because students, and students' families, feel themselves to be in a teacher's debt, not—as one might expect—to encourage favourable examination results. This matter of debts and obligations goes deep. Present-giving is its most obvious outward sign. But there must be an appropriateness, a balance. If a present is too lavish and expensive, the recipient is put in the awkward position of having incurred *giri*—the duty to return favours received. The debt of gratitude, 'for services rendered', as it were, is *on*. The interplay of *on* and *giri* may start a chain of giving and receiving which has been known to lead to financial ruin. But, happily, the balance is usually kept. Etiquette is observed with a good grace.

It has too, of course, its less winsome side: it was a Japanese who wrote, 'Our etiquette begins with learning how to offer a fan and ends with the rites for committing suicide.' The compartmentalism of Japanese life, with its almost watertight structure of separate and distinct behaviour in separate and distinct circumstances, can be not only puzzling but stifling and even abhorrent to the foreigner. The contrast between public and private behaviour, for example, is sometimes so wide that one cannot imagine that the same people are involved: this grim-jawed, heaving, kicking mob fighting its way into an underground train, for example—are these the same hosts who bow you into their houses with an elaborateness that would be tedious if it were not so obviously the formal mask on top of a genuinely hospitable face? Or these moon-viewing or public-garden-visiting crowds, scattering tangerine peel, lunch-boxes, beer bottles, cigarette ends and grosser trash on every favourite hilltop and urban grass-blade in the

20

country—are these, individually, the same people who keep the tiny sand paths to their houses scrupulously swept, and who are so attuned to visual balance that they will spend hours arranging a sprig of blossom and two twigs in a bowl?

The answer to both questions is: Yes, they are the same people. The Japanese have the best-adjusted set of stock reactions of any people I know, but the reaction must be fitted to its appropriate action. Get drunk at a party, especially if you are a poet: fine, it's expected of you, everyone will enjoy the expected absurdities. But, if you are a woman travelling with children, don't expect any man on the crowded bus to get up and offer a seat: your children will probably be offered as many seats as are necessary, and once seated they can kick and make themselves nuisances as much as they like, but, in this situation, you as a woman are not there—you will notice the men registering that you are not there. There are no beggars in Tokyo, officially, so no beggars exist, except for the licensed, maimed, and uniformed military veterans you see outside some of the big railway stations, to whom it is appropriate to give some money. But watch a Tokyo crowd passing an unlicensed, unmilitary beggar on the pavement (I remember particularly a ragged mother, her head bowed down to the stone and her two similarly ragged infants snuggling up to her like kittens, in the Ginza one day), and you will see no one even take in the existence of such a person, let alone give any money. The eye chooses to see what is fitting, what fits into the prescribed pattern, and whatever lies outside that is unthinkable, unseeable.

It is this sort of reasoning that makes some psychologists and anthropologists account for Japanese brutalities in war. In war, with its breaking-down of prescribed rules of action, prescribed rules of behaviour break down in their turn; and with the frustrations and hysteria which always lie just under the surface of Japanese life, feeding on poverty, overcrowding, the traumatic break (among boys, anyway) between childhood indulgence and the social strictness that comes down like a flail at puberty—with these suddenly thrown awry, the system breaks down and the man becomes a sadistic brute. This is an over-simplification, of course, and one ought to relate Japanese wartime behaviour towards the enemy to Japanese behaviour (both pre-war and during the war) within the army in general, where lieutenant slapped sergeant, sergeant slapped corporal, corporal slapped private, and the private bided his time until such a supremely slappable, kickable, whippable non-person as a foreign prisoner came into range. But never expect a Japanese to give you a rational—or, indeed, any—explanation of the Burma railway or the Rape of Nanking; for unless the man you question was there (in which case he will probably not reveal the fact), it is impossible for him to answer, because life has never presented him with a collapse of this sort. He cannot answer because he does not know.

A lot of nonsense has been talked and written in the West about 'The Way of the Samurai', 'The Knights of Bushido', and the like, generally by people who have a lip-smacking obsession with sadism. Far more apparent in Japan today is what one might with almost equal inaccuracy call 'The Way of the Sensei'. A *sensei* is a wise man. If you address a teacher, you call him *sensei*, not *san* (the usual word for 'Mr'); but equally a doctor of medicine, a priest, a master hairdresser, a master carpenter, a poet—all are *sensei*. It can have something to do with age—'the venerable', as it were—but not necessarily. What it implies more than that is devotion to some particular skill, an adeptness which the world recognises as the man's special gift. So the art of the poet-*sensei* is acknowledged and encouraged, and a poet at a social gathering is expected to produce a poem (usually written with the brush on rectangular strips of card which look rather like thick wallpaper samples). Because of this respect for the *sensei*, the teacher—of anything—is shown a deference rare in other countries. If it is known that someone does a bit of flower-arrangement, or dancing, or plays a musical instrument, the first question is, 'Who is his teacher?' Skills, it is felt, must be taught, and even pleasure must be disciplined. The Japanese response to beauty is partly a response to order, ceremony, the handing-on of precepts: which is perhaps why the Japanese are great codifiers, tabulating the best scenic views, for example, because some *sensei* at one time or another said that this was the finest vantage point for seeing such-and-such a mountain.

22

Hand in hand with this taught response to beauty goes a respect for practicality. The Japanese have imitative and ingenious eyes, and it is this that has made them such successful technological rivals of the West. The long years of Tokugawa isolation, following the centuries of absorption from China and Korea, opened out into a bewildering flood of notions, machines, gimmicks and luxuries from Europe and America after 1868. But the bewilderment did not on the whole take the form of foolish eclecticism, a mindless grabbing of whatever was new. The practicality of the Japanese is deeper based than that. Instead, they took what they wanted, what seemed necessary to them, adapted if it seemed best to do so, and rejected the rest. The craze for wearing bowler hats with kimonos did not last long, but beef and whiskey are still popular. The camera was taken up, copied, developed, improved—in the end—beyond western models. But neither the camera nor the typewriter have replaced skill with the brush, whether figurative or calligraphic—all go on side by side. The Germans trained the post-Meiji Restoration army, the British the navy, and within thirty-odd years Japan, until lately a medieval society with bows and arrows, had trounced both China and Russia on the battlefield. This period, continuing until the late nineteen-twenties, was the era of 'the gallant little Nips', a condescending phrase which carried with it the concomitant that they were 'clever as monkeys'—with the implication that they looked like them, too. One hears less of this sort of thing nowadays, with Japan a world competitor in medical science, shipbuilding, textiles, cameras, radios, cars, canned goods, nuclear physics, and a whole range of other things. Their ingenuity has carried them beyond imitation, and they are much too clever—and much too successful—to merit condescension.

Modern urban Japan is full of noise, bustle, restlessness, neurosis, ugliness. The way from Haneda, Tokyo's airport, to the city is a depressing jumble of squalor and vulgarity, whether one goes by car or monorail. The drive in from the docks at Yokohama is even worse. Yet at the core of Japan, beyond the frenetic activity, is a deep peace: again, a taught and schooled virtue, a deliberate withstanding of a metropolitanism that is no more than a hundred years old. A Japanese office-worker, spruce with suit and briefcase, travelling to and from work in bus or train or his own car, concerned all day with dictaphones, telephones, adding machines (though if he works in a bank or a shop he may still use an abacus), returns to his house in the evening; and immediately he is absorbed into a pattern which, in essence, was already old at the time of the Meiji Restoration. He has a scaldingly hot bath in a deep, wood-lined tub, in water which the rest of the family will use after him—decent enough, since he will have washed and rinsed himself *before* getting into the bath. Then he will change into a *yukata*, thick or thin according to the season, and sit on the rice-matting at a low table where a few small pickled vegetables and a bowl of green tea are laid for him. He may watch television or listen to the radio, but he is just as likely to write a poem; and even the television screen may show him a *sumo* match, 'the wrestling done to please the gods', which is traditionally traced back to 23 BC. The office-worker's daughter may be learning the *samisen* or the *koto*—or the piano—in another room. In that other room there may be some foreign-type chairs, a wooden floor, a cocktail cabinet, and a rather laboured imitation of a French Impressionist painting. But the man's relaxation, the life into which he naturally enfolds himself at home, is likely to be deeply and unmistakably Japanese.

In the city he has left, now given over to the night, there will be a mass of inconsistencies, or a mass of pleasurable choices, whichever way you want to look at it. In the areas of Asakusa and Shinjuku the bars and the little theatres will be open: bars which may range from a couple of wooden benches and a rough table to opulent affairs with concealed strip lighting and Mozart or Bartok on the long-player; and theatres where the main focus of attention may be a *danmari*, a balletic sword-fight between medieval warriors, the stage at the end piled with corpses like some parody of a Jacobean tragedy. Along the Ginza and Nihonbashi, the skyline will be a flaring, wriggling mass of neon advertising, and the big department stores (Takashimaya, Mitsukoshi) will still be open, with their uniformed girls at the doors and at top and bottom of the escalators, bowing and whispering '*Irasshai*' ('welcome') and other blandishments and

24

encouragements in a tiny sing-song undertone. Cinemas are everywhere—Japan has the biggest film industry in the world—but the visitor from abroad should not expect an unending diet of Ozu and Kurosawa, for these distinguished directors and their output represent only a small proportion of films released, good, bad, and indifferent. One is as likely to see a fourth-rate piece of Japanese Wardour Street-medieval, with many swords and much blood, or a comedy about wartime rookies in the army, or a domestic epic on soap-opera lines.

Only those with a lot of money—generally on company expenses—will be dallying with one of Japan's best-known features: the *geisha*. These girls, and women, still survive with every sign of vitality, but they must be thought of as elaborate and expensive items of entertainment, purveyors of innocuous pleasure in the crafty game of getting a contract signed or swinging a bloc of votes. Certainly they aren't prostitutes, in any usual sense, though many of them are what our ancestors would have called 'kept women'. As apprentices, usually in their middle teens, they are known as *maiko*, and they are subject to a discipline as strong as that of any nunnery. They practise the *samisen*, the *koto*, flutes and drums; they must be adept at every sort of game, from *go* (a kind of chess) to childish nonsenses involving butting balloons; they must be able to sing, recite, and be up in all the government and business gossip and scandals; they must be good listeners, they must move well, they must be perfectly groomed, and they must be beautiful—though the 'classical' Japanese beauty, with large chin, high forehead, thin smile, white matt skin and an expression compounded of pride and superciliousness, is not much to modern Anglo-American taste. The harmless frivolities of a *geisha* party easily lapse into boredom, unless one has a strong stomach for harmless frivolities.

There are, of course, more *avant-garde* pleasures than this. Japan was a natural soil for the transplanting of the Theatre of the Absurd, and has even managed some theatrical absurdities of its own. I once attended the rehearsals of an amateur 'new dance' group, held in what might, in British terms, have been a Territorial Army drill-hall: a hangar-like building, full of dust, peeling paint, and instructional charts. To the accompaniment of a random composition for saxophone and flute, a short-legged, horse-faced girl, completely naked but painted red down one side of her body and white down the other, performed some equally random steps. At intervals, a stage-hand—or so I supposed him—scuttled out into the acting arena to insert a marble, now under her armpit, now up her anus. The marble always, predictably, fell out. The 'dance' ended with the girl climbing on to a kitchen sink-unit (not a visual pun, surely?), and turning on the taps. Anything you can da I can dada better.

In the same way, a minority of Japanese have gone in for mud sculpture, concrete poetry, and 'happenings'. But again the Japanese spirit asserts or manifests itself. The border between poetry and calligraphy has always been a blurred one in Japan, the patterns of the *kanji* merging into fanciful or abstract shapes, so that concrete poetry is not quite the typographical foolery, or solemn nonsense, it often appears to be in countries which use the Roman alphabet. Or take the way in which some Japanese have adapted *ikebana* (flower arrangement) to modern terms of reference. At the Sogetsu *ikebana* school at Aoyama in Tokyo, one sees—within a building which itself is experimental, designed by Kenzo Tangé, one of the leading modern Japanese architects—a series of 'flower' arrangements which employ bits of metal and wire, bits of tortured wood, bits of machinery, like some mechanised parody of the traditional placing of blossoms and leaves in their ordained pattern of reconciliation: Earth, Man, and Heaven. Yet it is not intended as parody but as a grave coming-to-terms with the new. The old is still there, sanctifying the activity and the pattern.

'Sanctifying' is perhaps a curious word to use of a culture that has no idea of sainthood, and indeed very little that makes sense, to a foreigner, as religion. The anomalous and apparently casual blend of Shinto, Buddhism (with its Zen peripheries), Confucianism and pantheism that make up the religious attitudes of the Japanese is a stew best left to the expert to comment on. The post-war emergence of such eclectic faiths as *Tenrikyo* is typical: for *Tenrikyo* embraces a pantheon of gods, among whom are numbered Jesus, Confucius, Buddha, the prophet Muhammed, and Victor Hugo, whose naked statue adorns the sect's chief shrine. Yet, though one is amused by these absurdities, the great temples of Japan bear solid witness to a kind of faith which cannot have been lightly held. Some of them impress with their size, some with their interior decoration and design, some with their setting. The wealth, effort and devotion that went into them matches anything in Gothic Europe, and almost as striking is the carefulness with which many of them have been re-built after disasters of fire, earthquake and war. They are, in one strict sense, temporal structures, because they have always traditionally been built of wood, the basic Japanese material, yielding to every Japanese disaster. They are not magnificent examples of religious architecture, in the way that York Minster or Chartres are magnificent, but their very flimsiness underlines what is peculiarly Japanese about them. They are products of that same resilient poverty which Kawai Kanjiro esteems in pots.

And the temples of Japan are essentially related to their surroundings. In the large cities some of them have lost this relationship, as office blocks and railway stations have crowded up against their compounds: it is difficult to detach this western urbanisation from the Asakusa Kannon temple in Tokyo, or the Nishi-Honganji in Kyoto. But elsewhere the blending of trees, moss, stones, water, has survived, so that the whole 'inscape'—and Gerard Manley Hopkins, who invented the word, would have relished these temples—is balanced as a composition. The great architects and the great landscape designers worked together; sometimes both functions were combined in one man. Even the simplest temples usually have this balanced composition, the *torii* with its austere lines having something of the same function as the Greek propylon, but, unlike the propylon, quite without any attempt to erect steep and unassailable limits between sacred and profane: it is an entrance through which you walk unhindered, not a symbolic wall of columns shunning the vulgar.

Domestic architecture has the same simplicity. Though more and more big blocks of flats are built in the cities, the natural and desired place for a Japanese to live is the one-storeyed wooden house with its own patch of land, however small. The suburbs of Tokyo are full of such houses, set away from the main roads, by lanes which are unmetalled, dusty in summer,

27

muddy in winter. To live in they are not at all well-suited to the Japanese winter, but in summer one sees the point of this 'open house' plan: the outer walls slide back so that house and garden almost become one. And it is the garden—which may be no more than a tiny patch of ground—that is the focus of the house. In it there will probably be a small pool, or at least an earthenware vessel set in the ground and filled with water; perhaps a stone lantern; some *bonsai* or dwarf trees; and stones set cunningly about, creating an illusion of space within the limits.

Inside the house there is often—despite all one sees in magazines devoted to domestic design and in architectural journals—an inevitable feeling of clutter and temporariness: holes in the paper screens, things piled up on the floor rather than put in cupboards. No one should imagine that Japanese houses have a pure, unlived-in symmetry, or that they are easier to keep clean and tidy than western houses. But what can almost everywhere be found is the scrupulous taste and appropriateness of the scroll and seasonal flower arrangement placed in the *tokonoma* or alcove of the main room. If the garden is the focus of the house, the focus within the house is the *tokonoma*: to sit in front of it is to sit in the place of honour.

Perhaps because of the frenzied public clangour of Japanese cities, the house is seen as a refuge more than it is elsewhere. So is the restaurant, which is not normally a place where one eats in public to the accompaniment of twenty competing conversations but is a series of separate rooms, where couples or private groups—or, indeed, the solitary—are served with individual attention, in a setting of gardens, the sound of spring water, and a deliberate composure. The chief purpose of a Japanese house seems to be to cultivate calm, and this is an old theme of poets, as in several of Tachibana Akemi's 'poems of solitary delights':

> *What a delight it is*
> *When on the bamboo matting*
> *In my grass-thatched hut,*
> *All on my own,*
> *I make myself at ease.*

Tachibana died in 1868, the year of the Meiji Restoration, so that his reference to his 'grass-thatched hut' was probably genuine. In a town-poet of modern times it would have to be taken as a fanciful archaism. But despite Japan's urbanisation and industrialisation, the country is still seen as the 'real' Japan, and townee Japanese are assiduous in visiting it. It is the raw material of their painting, their poetry, and their pleasure. As the great seventeenth-century *haiku* master Bashō wrote:

> *The beginning of art—*
> *The depths of the country*
> *And a rice-planting song.*

So the twentieth-century Japanese tries to create his *rus in urbe*, or replenishes himself by visiting the country.

But here is a paradox. He is unlikely to make his expeditions alone but will band together with old school friends, relatives, some set of possibly like-minded people; for the Japanese are not natural solitaries. They have group attitudes and they love being organised in groups. Big firms—banks and factories—organise holidays for their employees in specially-made holiday houses in the country, where groups of co-workers are despatched together. Holiday camps of this sort existed in Japan before Billy Butlin, though they seem to lack the heartiness and raucousness of the British variety. Swimming, skiing, hiking, the viewing of autumn leaves— these are communal activities. At railway stations a common sight is a band of holiday-makers, often with identifying arm-bands, clustering round the group leader, who carries a flag which he waves above his head from time to time in order to attract his followers' attention and to keep them together. This sort of herding is bred into a Japanese from a very early age, for the schools act in this way, organising mass visits to the Daibutsu at Kamakura or the National Museum at Ueno. (School overcrowding accounts for some of this: a proportion of children has to be out of the schools at any one time, otherwise there are not enough classrooms to go round.) In the same way, one can still see bus-loads of visitors (mainly elderly women from the country) being disgorged from buses outside the Imperial Palace grounds in Tokyo, to look across the moat and perhaps to bow. Even Fuji, beautiful at a distance but a mere cone of cinders when one climbs it, is ascended by hordes of dutiful nature-pilgrims. Tachibana's pleasure in relaxing 'all on his own' seems, when one looks at Japan in some moods, wistfully poetic rather than realistic.

Yet despite Japan's dense urban population, its sometimes almost suffocating feeling of crowdedness, its jostling gregariousness, it is possible without travelling too far to find the rural calm and isolation which the poets celebrate. Hokkaido, the northernmost of the four main islands, is still thinly populated, given over to great forests and streams, paddies and pasturage. This is the dampest and coldest part of the country, and for that reason is not the first place a Japanese thinks of for his holiday. Here are the dairy farms, steadily increasing as the people develop a taste for milk, butter, and cheese. The northern and western areas of Honshu, the main island, are still largely unspoiled, with the so-called 'Japan Alps' running as a spine down the middle: the Japanese have a habit of labelling their most splendid natural features with foreign names (e.g. 'the Uchigawa Rhine'), but one has the feeling that this is for foreign tourist purposes. Japan has no need of it, just as to call Edinburgh 'the Athens of the North' diminishes rather than adds to the splendour of the city. Yet inevitably, and pleasurably, one is reminded of familiar scenes. Nojiri-ko, for example, a lake beyond Nagano to the north-west of Tokyo, may suggest parts of Canada, or New Zealand, or Norway, or even the English Lake District. Yet the tiny hamlet at the far end of the lake from the holiday-village of Nojiri could be nowhere but in Japan: it can be reached only by boat or by tracks across the mountain (if there is a fire, the fire-engine must go by boat from Nojiri), and the silkworm cultivation which is the basis of the people's life continues in the old primitive way. Close by, in the village of Kashiwabara, is the birthplace of Kobayashi Issa, the eighteenth-century poet who ranks with Bashō and Buson as the finest *haiku* writer; and his poems, with their sharp juxtapositions of the macrocosm and the microcosm, are true reflections of this landscape, with its mountains, forests, lakes, its rich and swarming natural life:

> *With bland serenity*
> *Gazing at the far hills:*
> *A tiny frog.*

> *Far-off mountain peaks*
> *Reflected in its eyes:*
> *The dragonfly.*

Even the Inland Sea, the long sleeve of water separating southern Honshu from the islands of Shikoku and Kyushu, is, despite its reputation as a holiday area, large and various enough to absorb its tourists. And close to Tokyo wild and lonely landscapes are to be found. In the Izu peninsula, only a little over sixty miles from the capital, there are the garish and popular spas of Atami and Ito, favourite places for clandestine weekends, full of hot springs, hotels, and scandal; but go beyond them, into the centre or the western coast of the peninsula, and you find mountains and trees which must have changed little since the poet Oshikochi Mitsuné wrote, in the early ninth century:

> *The end of my journey*
> *Was still far off,*
> *But in the tree-shade*
> *Of the summer mountain*
> *I stood, my mind floating.*

This 'floating world', this 'world of dew', as the old Japanese writers called it, summing up in that phrase the impermanence of nature and of human life, brings me back to the concept of *awaré*, to consider it again after stressing its importance as part of the Japanese concern with the ephemeral, the pessimistic, even the gloomy. Modern Japanese writers have embraced almost

31

too eagerly the doom-laden novelists and poets from abroad, so that *The Waste Land*, for example, influenced the post-war literary generation as strongly in Japan as it did western poets rather earlier: one annual anthology of new poetry is called *Arechi* ('Wasteland'), and there are seven different translations of the poem. Gloom is too often equated with profundity, and one of the leading writers of the early twentieth century, Noguchi Yoné, wrote: 'I should like to know where is a Japanese poet who is not sad.' Yet it would be wrong to accept this melancholy, whether genuine or—as it sometimes is—fashionably adopted, without pointing out that there is also a strong fund of common sense and common good humour. There is even a considerable amount of satire, though some Japanese intellectuals affect the opinion that it is not native to Japan. If they are thinking of the difficulties of response Japanese students have when confronted with, say, eighteenth-century English verse satire, in the shape of Pope, they are right, of course; but such difficulties are not exclusively Japanese. They forget, or minimise, the work of their own seventeenth-century writer Saikaku, who deals with the lives, presumptions and follies of the new merchant class, and combines documentary with sharp social comment—implied more often than stated, but that is part of his skill.

Even more neglected by 'serious' critics has been that type of verse known as the *senryu*: written in the same seventeen-syllable verse-form as the *haiku*, but substituting realism for fancy or whimsy. Taking their name from Karai Senryu (1718–90), these poems have flourished ever since, but they are almost always anonymous, and are usually regarded as being beneath academic dignity, not to be taken seriously as literature, and as holding a place which perhaps corresponds to the limerick and the clerihew. It has on the whole been left to foreigners (such as R. H. Blyth, an Englishman long resident in Japan, and also an assiduous translator of *haiku*) to rehabilitate them. Some examples of a few early *senryu* will give the flavour:

> '*She may have only one eye*
> *But it's a pretty one*',
> *Says the go-between.*

Zen priest,

Meditation finished,

Looking for fleas.

A horse farts:

Four or five suffer

On the ferry-boat.

A letter from a man

She doesn't much care for—

Showing it to mother.

What is apparent here is an acuteness, a mordancy, and a nice spirit of tough self-deflation, all of which are refreshing after the austerity, gloom, or insubstantialness of much Japanese art. The go-between in a marriage compact, Zen, the river scene, love letters—all these are themes which a *haiku* poet could deal with in his verse, but they would have to be tied to their season-word (all *haiku* must observe the convention of referring somehow to the season at which the poem was written), and they would have to be taken 'seriously'. The *senryu* about the horse and the ferry-boat, in fact, is a deliberate puncturing of the expected mood.

But what is aimed at is as resonant in juxtaposition as any *haiku*: the mating of appropriate but unexpected coincidences. These are *senryu*, modern and anonymous:

In the policeman's arms

The lost child points

Towards the sweet-shop.

The winter fly

Weakly collides

With the sliding doors.

And these are *haiku*, both by the revered Issa:

> *The radish-picker*
>
> *With his radish*
>
> *Points the way.*

> *Stop! don't swat the fly*
>
> *Who wrings his hands,*
>
> *Who wrings his feet.*

Here Issa observes the conventions (radish suggests spring, fly suggests summer), but the humanity for which he is famous makes him come very close to the spirit of the *senryu*. Japanese rule-making in the arts, which at first sight seems to be so thorough and categorical, in fact is open to exceptions. Even in the *Noh* theatre, the slow pace and more than Sophoclean sense of burdened 'necessity' is relieved by the *kyogen*, the 'mad words' or interludes in which farce and even horseplay is the keynote: for example, someone expostulating about a third person to his friend, while in the course of his ranting the friend goes away and the third person comes up unnoticed and hears everything.

That great wrong-headed enthuser about things Japanese, Lafcadio Hearn, wrote a notably off-putting essay on 'The Japanese Smile'; but the Japanese laugh can be as visceral and uninhibited as the next man's.

Laughter can sometimes be found in circumstances which seem inappropriate to westerners, particularly as an embarrassed mask for sadness. It is considered bad form to introduce one's own misfortunes to another; if the hearer is saddened, then the bearer of misery is in his debt. So when I asked a girl who began to work in the house for us whether her parents were alive, she told us with great gusts of laughter that they had both been killed in the 1945 fire-raids on Tokyo. The laughter was meant to show us that we should not sympathise: here was something which, she was suggesting, affected her alone, and should be no concern of any sympathy of ours. The Japanese, for all their stoicism and impassivity—that 'inscrutability' which is so readily attached as a label by foreigners—are nevertheless an extremely emotional people; but if possible there must be an objective correlative for their emotion. I remember a student at some university social occasion standing up and saying, among the other encomiums loaded on me as being appropriate to his teacher, that he had been moved to tears by my reading of Nashe's poem 'In time of plague' earlier in the term. At a Kabuki play the tears flow freely, just as at a baseball match between two popular teams (baseball is the most eagerly followed game in Japan) the demonstrations of support and excitement are quite extravagant. When one reads that the Japanese commander at Nanking wept when he heard what his troops had done, one's reaction is likely to be impatient and cynical; yet his was a wholly imaginable Japanese response—as imaginable as the behaviour of those troops.

A good deal of Japanese emotional energy goes into their patriotism, but one should not confuse that with the militaristic chauvinism of the nineteen-thirties and the war years, which was largely the result of economic frustrations carefully cultivated and channelled by empire-building generals and admirals: the Greater Asian Co-Prosperity Sphere had a heady ring, though there was both practical and idealistic opposition to it. The real patriotism of Japan is enshrined in the word *kokushin* with which I began: it can be found as early as this poem by the Emperor Jomei, who reigned from AD 629–41, called 'Climbing Mount Kagu':

> *In the land of Yamato*
>
> *The mountains cluster;*
>
> *But the best of all mountains*
>
> *Is Kagu, dropped from heaven.*
>
> *I climbed, and stood, and viewed my lands.*
>
> *Over the broad earth*
>
> *Smoke-mist hovers.*
>
> *Over the broad water*

Seagulls hover.

Beautiful, my country,

My Yamato,

Island of the dragonfly.

Here religion, legend, and a strong sense of natural beauty combine. The myths of the creation of Japan and of the founding of the Imperial line were taught as history until the 1945 defeat, and these myths—of divine volcanic eruptions, of the sun goddess and the sword god—may be seen either as the origin or as the product of an island people's awareness of its good fortune, its separateness, and its special skills. To the ordinary Japanese it must have seemed appropriate that the Emperor was a divinity, and though Hirohito maintains that he never fostered this notion, and has certainly been stripped of his godly trappings so that nowadays his life is as dull and powerless as that of any other constitutional monarch's, it is natural that the Japanese should have bestowed some of their passionate emotional attachment to their country on to the anciently-descended symbol of it.

Yet Japan, for all its ancient history, its awareness at every turn of that history in place-names, local legends, re-tellings of obscure feuds and loyalties in plays, films and popular novels (one of the most popular of these in recent years has been yet another version of the *Heiké Monogatari*, 'The Tale of Heiké', the original of which appeared in 1233), is in one curious way lacking in the stuff of ancientness: it has no ruins. This is partly due to the destructibility of Japanese building materials: wood and paper burn and leave no trace. If a damaged or destroyed building is thought worthy, it is re-built in replica. So there is no cult of traipsing round the remains, which is a pleasure that originated in Europe and has cast its net not only over Europe and the Mediterranean basin but also over Central and South America, the Near and Middle East, and several parts of the Far East. Japanese archaeologists are typically assiduous, well-informed, scientific and methodical, but what they can produce for the layman's delectation is small beer when compared with any other ancient civilisation in the world. There is the early

36

Jōmon pottery which turns up all over the place, no more and no less interesting aesthetically than other crude prehistoric ware; there are, rather later, bronze swords, spears and bells; and, most attractively, there are *haniwa*, the clay figurines, fashioned as men, horses, even monkeys, which were placed round ancient burial mounds. But the visitor will look in vain for any equivalent of the Parthenon, the Colosseum, the Pyramids, Cuzco, or Fountains Abbey.

This lack of ruins underlines one of the basic features of Japan: the continuity of its history. Ruins usually come about through the rejection, for one reason or another, of buildings which are in some way alien to succeeding people or ideas. The Old English poet who wrote 'The Ruin' saw the deserted remains of Roman Bath, was moved by them, but was not prompted to re-build what he saw. The Goths, the Vandals, the Arabs under Amr Ibn el-As, the Reformation despoilers of the great monastic houses—all plundered and, when they came to build, built differently. But Japan, despite civil war and clan feud, has for its whole recorded history been a homogeneous society; until 1945 it had never been invaded, conquered, or occupied. The result was a lasting pattern of habit, behaviour, and style of life, which even now is remarkably resilient. There is so strong a sense of the past and the past's inheritance in Japan that there is no need of ruins to act as concrete reminders.

So one comes back to this delicate balance between peace and violence, order and chaos, the uncertain stance of modern Japan. When Tokyo offered itself, and was accepted, as the home of the 1964 Olympic Games, the city was thrown into an upheaval of planning and construction such as it had not known since the war. New roads, stadiums, blocks of flats, hotels, came into being, and millions were spent on modernisation. What was at stake, evidently, was the reputation of Japan as a leading world power, capable of competing on equal terms not only athletically but as an up-to-date host. The test was passed triumphantly, but in the process, of course, something of the seedy, raffish charm of the former Tokyo was lost; that Tokyo which in Nagai Kafu's later stories and sketches seems to take on some of the atmosphere of Isherwood's pre-Hitler Berlin, with the dressing-rooms of variety halls, cheap all-night restaurants, bars, and prostitutes. Yet however efficiently streamlined modern Japan may be, with apparently no room for the makeshift and the temporary, even now it only needs a severe typhoon or (luckily a rare occurrence) a bad earthquake to remind you that the balance is indeed a delicate one.

It is the essential and irreducible Japan that is apparent in Roloff Beny's photographs, but what these photographs present survives not only in the camera's selective eye. 'Kimigayo', the Japanese national anthem, with its solemn, almost lugubrious tune, has the following words (in the 'official' translation by the nineteenth-century Japanophile Basil Hall Chamberlain):

> *Ten thousand years of happy reign be thine:*
>
> *Rule on, my lord, till what are pebbles now*
>
> *By ages united to mighty rocks shall grow*
>
> *Whose venerable sides the moss doth line.*

The sentiments are addressed to the Emperor, and come from an ancient poem. But they are in a deeper sense patriotic, in that they form an image of Japan as it is seen, revered and loved by its people: the pebbles growing into rocks and the rocks becoming lined with moss seem a metaphor of these narrow, ancient, fragmented, precarious, enduring islands.

When I think of Japan nowadays (and I am writing this in a Mediterranean landscape and in an Islamic culture that could not be more different from Japan), it is natural that I see in my mind's eye the small world I knew best, that suburb of west Tokyo where I lived. I think of the house itself, small, unpretentious, no different from thousands of other houses all over Japan; only five or six years old, yet a house in which (if one removed the useful excrescences of refrigerator and telephone) Tachibana Akemi would probably have felt at home. Here we scurried through the sliding screens into the garden whenever the thud and rumble announced an earthquake; a garden fenced with bamboo and fringed with pines. In the lane outside one could look south-west and see Fuji on a clear day, and down the lane, morning and afternoon, would come the *tofu* seller, a boy in baggy blue *mompei* with a white head-band round his forehead and a long yoke across his shoulders, from which hung wooden tubs of white beancurd—that humble, bland food which seems so typically Japanese in its purity and simplicity. At the end of the lane was a temple, hung with the red disc of the rising sun at New Year and festivals: we would be woken in the early hours of the morning by the sound of the temple drum, heavy, grave, gradually accelerating like a barrel rolling downstairs. In the plots of land between the houses, *daikon* (giant white radishes) were grown, manured with the night-soil collected by an old man with a cart. On the edge of the main road to Shibuya, down which the trams clanged and shrieked their claxons, stood an old farmhouse round which the suburb had spread. It was thickly thatched, and in its garden was the more stoutly-made traditional storehouse, which held the valuable *kimono* and other treasures, to be brought out only on special occasions. Along the street were the open shop fronts, displaying vegetables laid out on boards on the floor, the wares of the *tatami*-maker and the maker of paper lanterns, the rice shop with its big weighing-machines. And down a lane on one side was the abacus school, where at night rows of boys and girls rattled the wooden beads across the frames, so that they could be heard fifty yards away.

This blend of sights and activities, old and new, in an unexceptional suburb was and is typical of Japan. Behind it I see the grander landscapes of the country, the temples, the gardens, the scatter of tiny islands—almost all of them named and peopled with legend—and I see the individual faces of the people, no longer blurred into an unidentifiable mass as when first I saw them but separate and idiosyncratic. How presumptuous it is to select from all this material and say 'This is Japan'! If I were asked to show something which summed up in little the essence of Japan, I might think of a fine tea-bowl, a flower-arrangement, a *haiku*; yet these would be too delicate, they would leave out that staying-power, that deeply primitive sense of survival that marks the continuity of Japan, rising above typhoon, earthquake, fire bomb, atomic bomb. I should choose a poem by a modern poet, Kondo Azuma, written during the war. In it, as in the best of Japan today, the past and the present are reconciled, and the tough dignity and resilience of the Japanese are celebrated. The poem is called 'Fire':

The distant range of the mountains, like a shark's lower jaw,
Bared its fangs to heaven.
Shapes of people turning into crows.
Blackness of night covering everything.
No newspaper
No watch
But a vast expanse of bean-field.
I was flurried, as if I had strayed into the age of the gods.
But
Now and again the latest warplanes flew overhead in formation
And I heard the sound of Skoda machine-guns.

I asked
Do you have hope?
He did not reply.
What do you have?
He pointed to his garden:
There, stacked or scattered,
Was dried ox-dung.

What is that?
Fire!
Fire?
A cake of dung
Under a huge cauldron
Was burning, white, red.

He and I
For the first time laughed the laugh of god and man,
Laughed the laugh of god and man.

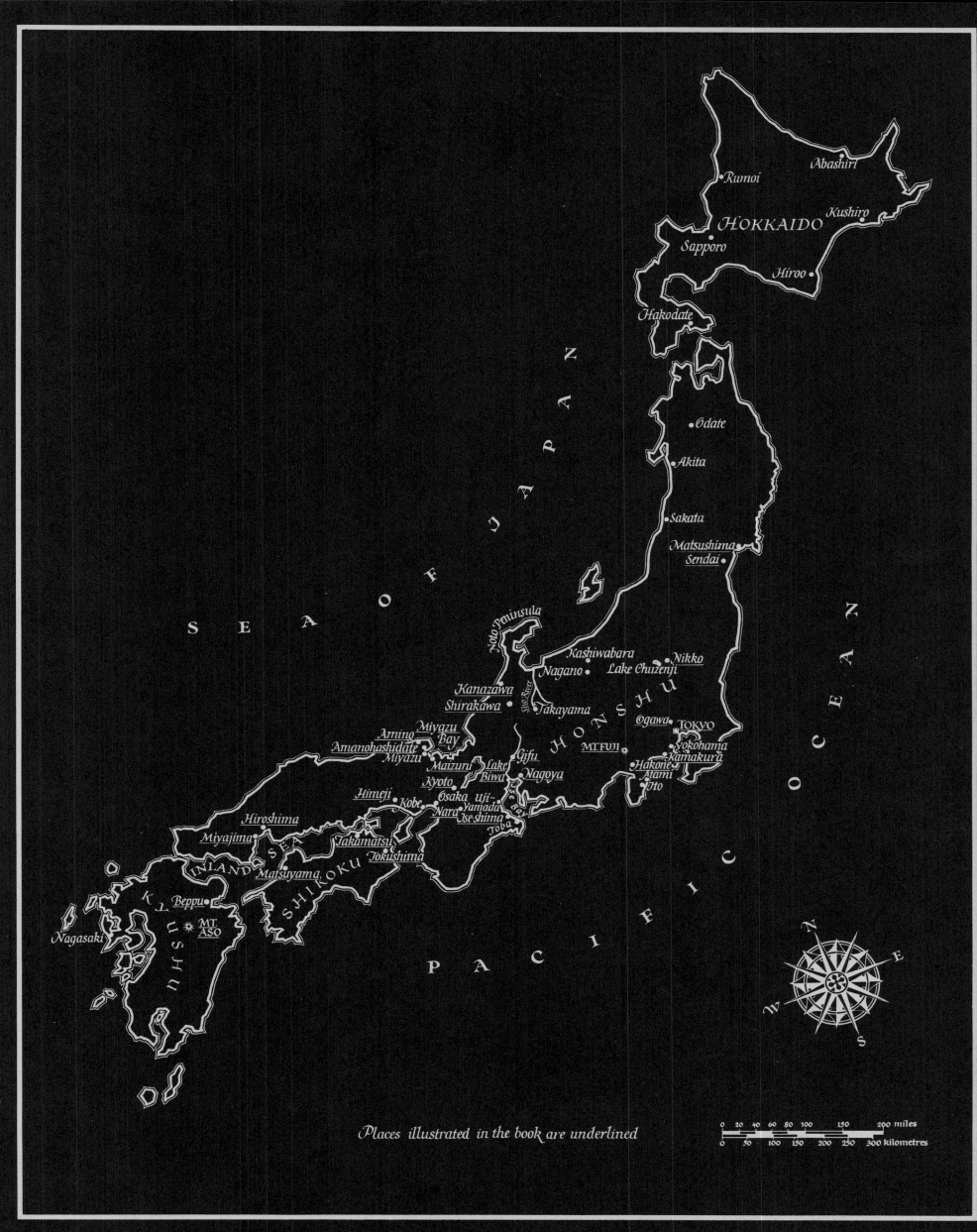

Places illustrated in the book are underlined

Images of a landscape

The great *torii* or shrine-gateway at Miyajima, near Hiroshima, is a fittingly symbolic gateway to Japan itself. Miyajima Island is traditionally one of the so-called 'Scenic Trio' of Japan, Amanohashidate and Matsushima being the other two. These three were first linked, and praised, by Hayashi Razan (1583–1657), a scholar of the Chinese classics. All are coastal sites and all are much visited, not least, one feels, because in the past a cultivated person gave them a title.

Itsukushima Shrine stands by the beach. Its history can be traced to very early times: there are records of its existence going back to the early ninth century AD. The main shrine has three parts: the innermost sacred area, where the three daughters of the Shinto deity Susano-o-no-Mikoto are reputed to live; a surrounding part where only the priests enter; and the outer area for public worship. These and the surrounding buildings of the shrine are in brilliant vermilion lacquer, and as the tide rises all seem to float on top of the sea. But even at low tide and in the evening light the shape of the *torii*, like some formalised piece of calligraphy, stands out, towering over fifty feet above the shore.

Though ancient in form and occupying the original site, it is typical that the Miyajima *torii* is a comparatively recent replica, the latest of a long line: it was built—of camphor wood—in 1875. The Japanese revere the spirit and symbolism of antiquity rather than antiquity for its own sake, and in a country of ephemeral wooden architecture it is not surprising that many 'old' buildings are in fact reconstructions, usually made with meticulous accuracy.

The ancient Shinto dances—*bugaku* and *kagura*—are particularly associated with the Itsukushima Shrine, and at festival times these are performed on a large open-air platform jutting out over the water in front of the shrine. A landscape of mountains and water, an architecture of symbolic forms, and dances of ritual significance compose a characteristically Japanese unity.

PLATE 1: *Torii*, Itsukushima Shrine, Miyajima

42

Such unity, too, can be found at the Jingu Shrines of Uji-Yamada. Here, in a peninsula south-west of Kyoto, is a National Park which covers the greater part of the provinces of Ise and Shima. The shrines which form a part of this park are important from the point of view of Japanese mythology: Kotaijingu or the *Naiku* (inner shrine) is dedicated to the sun goddess, Amaterasu-Omikami, who, in the version of Japanese history taught in the schools until the end of the second world war, was the parthenogenic product of the god Izanagi, one of the two original deities and the great-great-great-great-great-grandfather of the first Emperor of Japan, Jimmu, who ascended the throne in 660 BC. Hence the divinity of the Emperor, an official dogma which was discarded only when Hirohito made his famous renunciation in 1945.

The Myoto-iwa, or 'wedded rocks', are outliers of the main shrines, on the coast at Futami-ga-ura, four miles from Yamada. These rocks are popularly likened to Izanagi and his consort Izanami. The embraces of these two divinities (learned from watching two love-birds) resulted in the birth of a number of islands—the islands of Japan, the first islands in the world. So the story goes, or went. In the two rocks, the microcosm is taken for the macrocosm. The two are joined by a large straw-rope, which is replaced every year on January 5th at the end of the New Year Festival, Japan's chief holiday. On the larger of the two rocks (representing Izanagi) stands a *torii*, a smaller and simpler version of the great gateway at Miyajima.

No one need bother any more about the rather absurd mythology. But the composition itself—two unequal rocks joined by a simple strand—is satisfying and even evocative. Here, as in so many other Japanese settings, nature and art blend, so that one can hardly tell where one ends and the other begins.

The beauty and symbolism of water are important in any consideration of Japanese aesthetics: as a setting for the Itsukushima Shrine and the Wedded Rocks, where water is related to something man has done or made, or simply as natural background. In the Beppu district in Kyushu, the main southern island, there are many *jigoku* or boiling ponds, one of which—the Chinoike-jigoku or 'ruby pool'—has quite naturally been taken to be a representation of hell: it is vermilion in colour, is over 500 feet deep, and has a temperature of almost 170°F.

As a contrast, there is the cold stillness and placid monotone of part of the Sho River, not far from Shirakawa in north-central Honshu, where damming has resulted in the drowning of a forest: the result is so beautiful that it has become a favourite viewing place for Japanese, who find in its bare white branches, its chilly and delicate 'fixing' of tree, rock and water, a composition which appeals to their sense of *shibui*.

PLATE 3: Chinoike-jigoku, Beppu

PLATE 4: Sho River, near Shirakawa

The waters of hell
Steaming and fuming
Even in winter.

The drowned forest
Has lost all its leaves:
Even the water empty.

The Meiji Shrine, dedicated to the Emperor Meiji, who reigned as the first emperor of modern Japan from 1868 to 1912, is one of the holiest centres of pilgrimage in Japan. A grave, compassionate and astute monarch at a time of much excitement and confusion in his country, he was also a prolific poet, and is reputed to have composed more than a hundred thousand *tanka*—poems of thirty-one syllables built on the same syllabic structure as the seventeen-syllable *haiku*. As statesman, poet, and father of his 'new' country, the Emperor Meiji brought the monarchy and what it stood for back into repute; and the Meiji Shrine was the popular result of his country's devotion. The gardens cover almost 180 acres in central Tokyo.

In the Minami-no-ike or south pond of the Inner Garden, sacred carp and water-lilies come together in a mood of strength and frailty. The Japanese much admire toughness and resilience, and it is these qualities that the annual Boys' Festival celebrates each May 5th. The traditional name for this festival is *Shobu-no-sekku* or 'iris fete', a name typically Japanese in its play on two meanings: the *shobu* is a kind of iris, with long, narrow leaves resembling sword-blades, a fitting symbol for young manliness; at the same time, the word *shobu* can be written with different characters, when it means 'striving for success'. On the day of the festival boys carry these leaves, or wooden swords carved in the same shape, while their elders drink finely-chopped iris leaves mixed with *saké*.

But the most obvious outward sign of the Boys' Festival is the group of cloth or paper streamers fastened to bamboo or pine poles in the gardens of all houses where there are boy-children. These streamers are fashioned in the shape of the carp, and as the wind fills them they belly out like wind-socks, seeming to swim in the air and battle against the currents. There will be a large one for the eldest son, and they diminish in size until there is only a small one for the baby. The popular legend accounting for this is that the carp (like the salmon) fights its way upstream and up waterfalls, tenacious, determined, and in the end successful: hence—in the official view—'the encouragement of manliness, the overcoming of life's difficulties, and consequent success'. The carp is also very long lived.

48

Another feature of the festival, now less commonly observed, is the erecting of a stand in the house (rather similar to that used for the *Hina-Matsuri* or Dolls' Festival on March 3rd), on which are displayed dolls representing famous generals of the past, such as Toyotomi Hideyoshi, the sixteenth-century leader who is sometimes known as the Napoleon of Japan. Bows, swords and spears may also be displayed.

The origins of the festival are not known, but some say that it can be traced to a function observed at the court of the Empress Regent Suiko (AD 593–629), a contemporary of the Emperor Jomei who composed the poem 'Climbing Mount Kagu', quoted in the introduction. It became popular in the Edo period (1603–1868), and since the second world war it has—perhaps in deference to the new idea of sex equality—been designated more generally *Kodomono-hi*, or Children's Day, and is a national holiday. But equality or not, it is still very much the boys' day, and the brightly coloured carp fly in the wind with undiminished vigour. It was perhaps in some mixed mood of reverence for such vigour and regret for the loss of his country's youth—in the Sino-Japanese war of 1894 or the Russo-Japanese war of 1904—that the Emperor Meiji composed this *tanka*:

> *The young go off*
> *To the gardens of battle.*
> *Old men alone*
> *Guard our fields at home.*

The ordering of nature is the impulse lying behind much Japanese art. Yet the English herbaceous border or the Italian formal garden are alien to Japanese notions of such order: the result must seem somehow natural, as if man and nature worked together to produce an inevitable balance. The garden illustrated here shows the impulse interpreted most faithfully.

The Katsura Kikyu, or Katsura Detached Palace as it is generally translated, lies about three miles south-west of Kyoto, almost caught in the suburbs of the city. Work began on it in 1590, at the order of Toyotomi Hideyoshi, who built it for Prince Tomohito.

The place is noted equally for its garden and its buildings. It is perhaps here that one sees Japanese landscape gardening at its best, without extremes and quirks, on a large scale, but with characteristic proportions and taste. It is said that the garden was designed by Kobori Enshu (1579–1647), a master of *cha-no-yu* (tea ceremony), the man responsible also for the garden of the Kohoan of the Daitokuji Temple, and for those of the Kodaiji, Nanzenji and Chion-in Temples. He was one of the last of the long line of priests responsible for landscape design; in the Edo period such work passed to professional gardeners (*niwa-shi*). Some idea of the special regard in which he was held can be had from the story that when Kobori was commissioned to lay out the Katsura gardens he first made Hideyoshi promise three things: to put no limit on the amount spent, not to hurry the work, and not to see the garden until it was finished, lest any suggestions he made might harass Kobori in his single-minded concern.

The result is a triumph of ingenuity and restraint. Just as the palace buildings themselves (also designed by Kobori) seem no more than particularly chaste and elegant versions of ordinary Japanese domestic architecture, without ornateness and ostentation, so the garden seems only a larger and more various version of a Japanese suburban one. Trees, shrubs, lakes, stone lanterns, stepping stones, bamboo fences, tea pavilions—all form themselves into a series of separate vistas, already composed for the eyes. There is no single vantage point better than another: it is planned in such a way that wherever you stand the prospect seems right.

The Palace is now the property of the Imperial Household (which means that permission to visit—usually readily granted—must be asked from the Imperial Household Agency in Kyoto), and the buildings and gardens are kept up with that regard for exact conservation which is a mark of Japanese care for their important ancient properties. Nothing, one feels, has changed here since Kobori put the finishing touches to his work in the early sixteenth century.

54

PLATE 8: Garden of the Katsura Detached Palace, Kyoto

Stepping on a tendril,
A whole hill of dew
Begins to move.

Across the lake
I step uncertainly
On stones and shadows.

The influence of China on Japan has been basic, and there has existed for centuries a relationship compounded of unequal parts of homage, rivalry, affection, envy and emulation. Japanese propagandists in the nineteen-thirties were apt to call the Sino-Japanese war a family conflict, as between brothers, thus smoothing over much treachery and cruelty. But there is no doubt that a whole complex of Chinese skills and attitudes lies behind much of what one thinks of as characteristically Japanese.

The Mampukuji Temple is a solid example. It was established in 1659 as the headquarters of the Obaku sect of Buddhism, by Ingen, a Chinese priest of the Ming Dynasty. The structure of the temple is thoroughly Chinese: the main buildings are made of teak, which is not a native wood, and the story goes that the original teak logs drifted to the coast of Japan from Formosa or the mainland of China. All the sculpture in the temple was made by Endosei, a Chinese artist, at a time when Japanese sculpture was in decline.

This, then, is a late flowering, in isolation, of an influence which was at its strongest from the sixth to the tenth century AD. At this period Buddhism spread from China, took root, and exerted a shaping spirit on the arts and architecture. But the Chinese ideograms—the basis of the Japanese written language—were an even earlier arrival: it was in AD 285 that a Korean messenger brought to Japan a scholar named Wani who was learned in the Chinese classics and who remained at the Court as teacher to Prince Uji-no-Wakiiratsuko. The introduction of Buddhism in AD 552 gave a new impetus to Chinese studies, for all the Buddhist scriptures were in Chinese. It was not until the Kamakura Period, beginning in 1185, that Chinese culture was for the first time spurned as effeminate and 'un-Japanese', an attitude which, with the swing of the pendulum, has punctuated Japan's history.

But China cannot be treated so lightly. The elements of Japanese government, as well as language, literature, religion, and the visual arts, are inextricably bound up with Chinese example; and it is only with post-Meiji Japan that one finds the country turning anywhere else with any enthusiasm. The present tightrope that all Japanese politicians tread between overtures to China and uneasiness about offending the United States shows a basic modern conflict: is Japan to be an Asian power, linked by tradition to China, or a western one, rejecting not only Chinese communism but centuries of cultural influence?

58

The noting and recording of nature's moods, weathers, views and changes has been the chief job of Japanese artists, both visual and literary, from the beginning. The temper of Japanese art has never been one of abstraction or intellectualism, and 'man in landscape' has been the Japanese way of embodying the human. Auden's observation would be quite foreign to a Japanese:

> *To me, art's subject is the human clay,*
> *And landscape but the background to a torso.*

Yet it is man who has imposed his will on the landscape, and there are few parts of the country where one can see nothing but entirely natural scenery. Although only a tiny proportion of the land can be worked agriculturally, the hills are stripped of their wood and the rivers of their fish: the industriousness and foresight of the people ensures that what is taken is put to good advantage—there is little waste—but the reckless felling of the wartime period has meant that Japan now imports much timber, despite the fact that over sixty per cent of the country is covered by woodland; and the post-war loss of fishing grounds off the coasts of the Kuriles, Saghalien, Korea and Formosa has forced the fishing boats into intensive activity in Japan's home waters. The seas, rivers and hills of Japan are not the preserve of the rural aesthete. They have to earn their way, and the practicality of the Japanese attempts to make them do so. A proverb sums up this steady common sense: *hana yori dango* (dumplings before flowers, or as D. J. Enright has more memorably put it, 'bread rather than blossoms').

By the Japan Sea, the western coasts of Honshu, one can see the harvesting of both land and water. Here, in a landscape of low hills and paddies, painters have found their inspiration for centuries. These are not the grand, rugged aspects of Japan, its magnificent but useless mountains, its mysterious but sterile or vindictive volcanoes; it is an area tamed by man, worked by the sweat of his brow and with an aching back:

> The beginning of autumn:
> Sea and emerald paddy
> Both the same green . . .

but also

> Girls planting paddy:
> Only their song
> Free of the mud.

Fish and rice are the traditional staples of Japanese diet, and despite the increasing popularity of bread, dairy products and meat, they continue to be so. There are more than 1200 varieties of fish in the inland and coastal waters, and no Japanese meal is quite complete without at least a slice of raw fish, or a few flakes of dried fish. Rice is the most important crop, combining the advantages of needing little fertiliser (important in a country with few domestic animals or phosphates), yielding a large harvest, and being able to be grown year after year on the same spot; but it needs much unpleasant manual labour, often working knee deep in mud and water, and in the busy seasons of planting and harvesting the paddies are full of whole families at work—babies strapped to mothers' backs, old men and women gleaning.

Forty per cent of the population is still made up of families earning their living from farming, fishing or wood-felling, but as industry grows the numbers drop year by year. In Japan as elsewhere the drift is to the towns, away from the tedious, ill-paid, generally unmechanised work of the country.

Gardens and Temples:
The Grammar of Design

PLATE 15: Garden through temple window, Matsushima

Temples and gardens are so closely related to one another in Japan that they must be considered together. The aim in the design of both is to create a miniature landscape of the greater world outside, not slavishly imitating it but selecting and formalising as a painter does when confronted with a canvas. One cannot say that the garden is a 'setting' for the temple: temple and garden form an essentially unified composition.

The traditional features of a Japanese garden cannot be grouped under one heading, for the Japanese, with their love of categorisation and codification, have classified two general types and a succession of sub-types. The two general ones are the flat garden (*hiraniwa*) and the hill garden (*tsukiyama*). The hill garden uses slopes, often so slight as not to be hills at all, lakes, ponds, moving water; and the consequent need for space has meant that such gardens have needed the resources of a rich man or a rich sect. The Shukukeien at Hiroshima and the Ritsurin at Takamatsu are examples of gardens laid out at the expense of an individual or a municipality, the Golden Pavilion at Kyoto of one maintained in this fashion by a sect. The flat garden can more easily be adapted in a humbler way. Stones, trees, stone lanterns, water basins, sand—these are the materials on the palette of the designer of a flat garden. Their simplicity and austerity go hand in hand with the teachings of Zen, so that some of the most famous examples of flat gardens are found in the grounds of Zen temples and monasteries, such as those of the Ryoanji and the Daitokuji, both in Kyoto.

Each of the two styles is sub-divided into three forms: *shin*, *gyo* and *so* (elaborate, intermediate, abbreviated), ranging from the strictly formal to the wild—though even the wild in Japan is thoroughly and cunningly mastered by man. Each has a history of religious and mystical precept: the principles of religion were applied to the traditional rules for the construction of landscape gardens.

Shinto—the Way of the Gods—is the native cult of Japan, lying behind the later adoption of Buddhism and Confucianism. It enshrines much that is still a part of living Japan: reverence for nature and for ancestors, and a belief in a whole range of gods and attendant spirits rather than in monotheism. Combined with Buddhism —particularly with Zen—it has determined the design of temples, gardens, the symbolism of birth, marriage and death, the rites of purification, prayer, and thank-offering. Combined with Confucianism, it contributed those feelings of loyalty to the family and one's superiors which make up Japanese attitudes to duty, filial piety, and the paternalism (however suspect this may be to labour reformers) of the employer.

The pantheon embraces what have been called 'the eight million gods', of sea, rivers, winds, fire, mountains and volcanoes, trees and stones, and innumerable mythological or quasi-mythological men and women of the past; some of these latter are scarcely detachable from local folk-myth and do not have general acceptance. But over them all presides Amaterasu-Omikami (Great Heaven-Shining-Goddess): to some Shinto theologians, in fact, this deity is one, and 'the eight million gods' merely manifestations of her presence everywhere. But there is no dogma about this, and indeed to the monotheist—whether Muslim, Jew, or Christian—Shintoism may seem bewilderingly lacking in dogmatism: faith and belief are wordless, boundless, and implicit.

Of the two forms of Shinto, Jinsha Shinto is the more prominent in Japanese history and the more sinister to the westerner, because of its usual translation as 'State Shinto' or 'Official Cult'. Indeed, Shinto shrines of the sect were, until the reforms of 1945, maintained at the expense of the central or local governments; and the emphasis on the exclusively Japanese purity of the faith, on the divinity of the Emperor and therefore on the rectitude of his government, was carefully stressed by propagandists in the nineteen-thirties and during the war, so that not to follow the militarists was made to seem not only unpatriotic but impious. Yet the forcible disestablishment of Jinsha Shinto by the Americans has not caused a noticeable dropping away of support: there are over 15,000 priests, supported by local believers, and attendance at the big shrines, such as the Meiji, and the small ones, particularly at the New Year Festival, is popular. Everywhere one sees worshippers clapping their hands and making obeisance, giving offerings of money, flowers, or rice, buying charms, or—just as typically—photographing one another in front of the holy places. There is a sense in which the priest is a museum piece, a work of art set among works of art, the formalised human expression of an essentially passive faith: a sense in which he is a symbol, just as the screen behind him with its chrysanthemums is a symbol, of all that is static and hierarchical in Japan. But the simplicity enshrined in him and his surroundings is not anachronistic, even in a country as 'modern' as Japan.

The Kinkakuji Temple, or Golden Pavilion, lies at the foot of Kinukasayama in Kyoto, and is one of the most famous buildings of the Muromachi Period (1392–1573). It was originally built as the villa of a Court noble, and the garden was laid out for this purpose in 1394. But a few years later it was turned into a Buddhist temple, which it still remains, though the original buildings have been repeatedly burnt down and rebuilt. The last destruction by fire was in 1950, when it turned out that the cause was arson by a disgruntled or mad priest: this incident formed the germ of a notably unpleasant but brilliant novel by Japan's best post-war novelist, Mishima Yukio, *The Temple of the Golden Pavilion*. A new building, like all its predecessors an exact replica of the original, was completed on the same spot in October 1955.

The garden is reached through the Karamon Gate, in front of which is the Golden Pavilion, standing three storeys high and with a bronze phoenix on the roof. The small lake has a grove of maples on one side and a brook running into it, with an arbour near by, where an early owner of the villa before it became a temple, the Shogun Yoshimitsu, held his counsels of state.

The Golden Pavilion is closely linked with the Ginkakuji, or Silver Pavilion, in the north-eastern part of Kyoto. The Silver Pavilion was built about a hundred years after the Kinkakuji, and in imitation of it: it too began as a villa and not a temple. The chief feature here is the Togudo, a devotional hall in the garden, and in particular its tea-room, the model on which all later ceremonial tearooms are based: it is a small room of only four and a half mats (all Japanese floor-surfaces are measured in terms of mats, standard-sized blocks of *tatami*). *Cha-no-yu*, tea-ceremony, 'a religion of the art of life' as it has been called, began in the Muromachi Period, and Shuko, the fifteenth-century originator of it, reputedly designed the Togudo. The commonsensical and hard-headed westerner is sometimes understandably impatient at the quasi-religious elaborateness and theorising that has grown round this simple formula; but in the gardens of the Golden and Silver Pavilions, and in Shuko's own tea-room, it may seem to make sense, in a peaceful and ordered setting. Certainly the cult is practised with great devotion and seriousness by hundreds of thousands of ordinary Japanese even today. It may be a calming and gently sanctifying influence in a busy and distracting life.

Kyoto is a city of temples, and despite the natural hazards of fire many of them have survived without the necessity of such facsimile work as we see at the Golden Pavilion. By order of the American high command, the city was not bombed during the war, and so the most splendid of Japan's four ancient capital cities survived the disaster which destroyed so many shrines and temples elsewhere.

70

PLATE 18: Shadows on wall, temple at Matsushima

PLATE 19: Tree shadows, castle wall, Sendai

Everywhere one finds the theme of nature imitating art and art imitating nature. The accidental shadow-fresco on a temple seems to prefigure the work of screen-painters, while shadows on a cyclopean castle wall seem like a lithograph or an engraved aquatint on the stone. The elaborately carved unvarnished wood below the shadow attempts to mime it. The random play of shadows moves naturally from such scenes to *haiku*, as in these two late seventeenth-century examples:

Painting pines
On the blue sky,
The moon tonight.

Harvest moon:
On the bamboo mat
Pine-tree shadows.

Takamatsu is one of the chief ports on the Inland Sea, that long expanse of water lying between Honshu and the islands of Shikoku and Kyushu. Ritsurin Park stands there, on the site of the former villa of the Matsudaira family, one of the great clans of Tokugawa Japan. It covers an area of about 134 acres, and the design harmonises with the natural forest of pine trees which forms the background. Here trees, shrubs, water, bridges and pavilions come as close to the informal as one can find in a Japanese garden, yet even so one is aware of a shaping intelligence. The people on the bridge themselves form part of the design, as they cross the park to the museum, art gallery, zoo, or children's playground, all of which lie within the park's moat.

Naturalism is a feature of the Shugakuin's gardens too. The Shugakuin Rikyu (like the Katsura an imperial villa) was built for the ex-Emperor Gomizuno-o, encouraged by the Tokugawa Shogunate which had deprived him of his power, and was begun in the first quarter of the seventeenth century. The three large gardens which make up its grounds each contain a summerhouse, but the main emphasis is on relating the trees, lakes and streams to the background of Mount Hiei, at the foot of which they stand. Next to it, the Katsura is considered artificial, with the Shugakuin's man-made features hidden or transformed where such things are open and acknowledged at the Katsura. The lake of the Upper Garden is formed by making a big earth dam at the mouths of a number of mountain streams: the earth of the dam is retained by four tiers of stone walls which are concealed by three tiers of tall hedges, and the roundish top of the dam is covered with clipped shrubbery. There are deliberate contrasts of water, from the broad sweeps and curves of the lakes to the narrow rock-fringed channels of the streams feeding them. Elsewhere there are waterfalls and rills, and even rice paddies have been incorporated into the scheme. In this setting the abdicated Emperor turned to contemplation, entering the priesthood in 1651 and assuming the religious name of Enjo. Later the villa in the Middle Garden was established for his daughter, Princess Mitsuko, and then was converted into a temple, when the princess became a nun to pray for the soul of her father.

PLATE 21: Lake, Upper Garden of Shugakuin Rikyu, Kyoto   PLATE 22: Stream, Shugakuin Rikyu, Kyoto

The Saihoji Temple is in the western outskirts of Kyoto. It belongs to the Rinzai sect, one of the three main branches of Zen.

PLATE 23: Moss garden, grounds of Saihoji Temple, Kyoto

Zen, the contemplative offshoot or ancillary of Buddhism, was a product of the twelfth and thirteenth centuries in Japan. 'Salvation by meditation' and 'a divine emptiness' were and are its chief tenets, and in practice this has meant austerity, discipline, cultivation of will-power. It was a sect that found favour among the *samurai*, the warrior class, because of these useful military virtues, and as such it helped in the development of the idea of *Bushido* (chivalry), a code of conduct which—like so much else—was geared to new uses by the pre-second world war and wartime regime. But it would be rash to attempt anything more than this thumbnail sketch, because notions of Zen have now spread all over the world, and no doubt each disciple thinks that he has found the Buddha within. For the outsider the most obvious visual expressions of Zen are to be found in such gardens as those of the Ryoanji, the Daitokuji, and the Saihoji.

The garden of the Saihoji is famous for one unique feature: it is thickly carpeted and overgrown with many kinds of moss, so that the temple is popularly known as *Kokedera* (moss temple). This was designed by the priest Muso-Kokushi (also known as Soseki), who was Superior of the Tenryuji Temple at Arashiyama, not far from Kyoto. He lived from 1275–1351, and was noted for his garden designs elsewhere in Japan, for example at Kamakura, where the Shogun's court, many of them *samurai*, were among the earliest adherents of Zen.

Muso-Kokushi's designs were the product of the first wave of Zen influence on the construction of landscape gardens. The tendency was to reject richness of colour or form and to concentrate on flatness (it was at this time that the *hiraniwa*, the flat garden, was evolved), muted colours, stones and trees rather than moving water and flowers. Muso-Kokushi's moss garden follows this tendency to an extreme that is, however, not nearly so austere as words might suggest. The variousness, delicacy, even the sensuousness of the moss—which can be as smooth as silk or as lush as a thick pile carpet—is such that puritanism and self-indulgence seem to strive for the upper hand. Over it all lies that *sabi* (patina) which is one of the words associated with *awaré*, itself a Zen-like concept.

The Daitokuji Temple, in the northern part of Kyoto, is another of the important shrines of the Rinzai sect of Zen. Here the garden of the Daisen-in was formed by Soami, an eminent designer of gardens who died in 1525. The materials are simply raked yellowish-white sand, rocks of varying sizes, and low hedges. Seen through diaphanous bamboo screens, these elements seem to resolve themselves into an equation which might solve the mystery of Zen. Beside it, the splendours of the Horyuji Temple at Nara, the oldest existing temple in Japan—and perhaps the oldest wooden structure in the world—look almost ostentatious, coming from a Buddhist opulence and generousness of worldly response that stand in sharp contrast to the rigours of Zen.

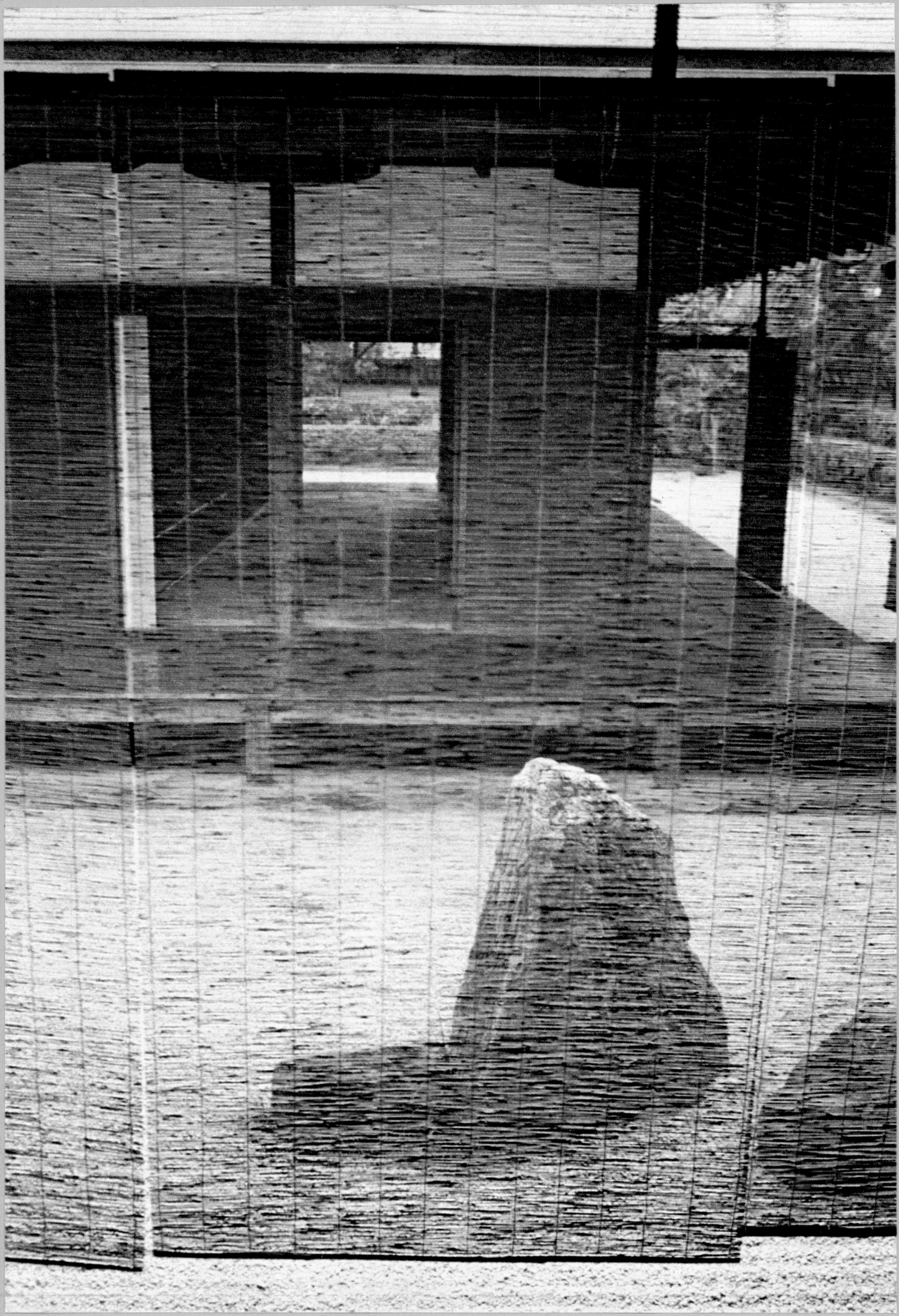

PLATE 24: Daisen-in, Daitokuji Temple, Kyoto

PLATE 25: Five-storeyed
Pagoda, Horyuji Temple,
Nara

Nikko, in a setting of mountains and thick deciduous forests, is the site of the chief secular shrine and the most elaborate architecture in Japan. Here, following his own instructions, the remains of Tokugawa Ieyasu (1542–1616), the founder of the Tokugawa Shogunate, were buried. Ieyasu's grandson, Iemitsu, carried out the work, which was completed twenty years after his grandfather's death.

It is a stupendous work. No expense was spared. An amount of gold-leaf that would cover six acres was used, 15,000 men worked on the buildings during the two years it took to make them, 50,000 bushels of rice were set aside annually to be sold to maintain the mausolea once they had been made. . . . The superlatives outstrip themselves. Yet, oddly, it all seems—at least to one visitor—alien to Japan. There can be little doubt that Ieyasu, for all his ability, was a megalomaniac (in the year of his death he conferred upon himself the title Tosho Daigongen, or the 'East-Illuminating Incarnation of Bodhisattva'), and seen in the light of other Japanese architecture the Nikko mausolea seem to bear an unhappy resemblance to such oriental follies as the 'Tiger Balm' gardens of Singapore and Hong Kong: the vulgar memorials of rich and tasteless men.

Yet of course one can be too severe about all this. Parts of Nikko are extremely beautiful. The Yomeimon, or Gate of Sunlight, is one example. Sometimes it is called the Higurashimon, or Twilight Gate, implying that its white and gold are best seen at twilight. The gate has two storeys and twelve columns; on the beams and rafter-ends are carved giraffes, dragons' heads, clouds, with lions' heads below. Flanking the entrance are gold *koma-inu*, lion-dogs of Chinese derivation, set among richly-carved tree and leaf forms, medallions of pines, bamboos, phoenixes, pheasants, cranes and wild ducks; and at the foot of the steps are bronze lanterns, again leaf-shaped in inspiration and again crowned with medallions.

All this magnificence at Nikko almost came to an end at the time of the Meiji Restoration, when some of the Tokugawa troops entrenched themselves in the buildings of the mausolea and prepared to defend them. Fortunately they were persuaded to evacuate and so saved the buildings from destruction. They are now constantly under repair, though not quite to the extent they were under the Shogunate, when it was the custom to repair them every twenty years: as the repairs themselves took ten years and the collection of material another ten years, the operation must have been like that traditionally associated with the Forth Bridge. Admission fees help to cover the modern repairs, and since Nikko is the most popular of all tourist places in Japan, among both Japanese and foreigners, the takings are considerable.

The cultivation, significance and symbolism of flowers and plants are linked with the religious and mystical importance of gardens. From the natural flower in its wild or garden state, through the formal forcing of blooms and leaves, to the making of artificial flowers out of paper and wax and the carving of them in wood or casting of them in metal—through all these runs a 'language of flowers' far more elaborate than anything practised in Renaissance Europe or Victorian England. The pine represents constancy, the bamboo prosperity, the apricot purity, the chrysanthemum the Emperor. . . . Japanese poetry is full of the imagery of flowers, from the 'cherry garlands' and 'sleeves white as mulberry' of the eighth century AD collection, the *Manyoshu*, to the 'moss flowers' and 'blossom-laden sky' of modern poets, who have disregarded the advice of their contemporary, Nakano Shigeharu: 'Don't sing of crimson flowers. . . . All that is delicate, all that is vague. . . . All that is elegant— out with it!'

The best-known manifestations of this concern with flowers are the importance attached to the cherry-blossom and to the cult of *ikebana* or flower arrangement. The *sakura* or cherry is open to three stock responses: it immediately suggests beauty, the season of spring, and the impermanence of life. Thus the seasons are enumerated in this *haiku*:

> *Cherries, cuckoo,*
> *Moon, snow—soon*
> *The year's vanished.*

There is the scarcely-to-be-expressed ecstasy at seeing the blossom:

> *Oh! oh! is all I can say*
> *For the cherries that grow*
> *On Mount Yoshino.*

PLATE 32: Shinto roadside cemetery, Japan Sea coast

And there is the spirit of *awaré* suggested in:

> *They bloom and then*
> *We look and then they*
> *Fall and then . . .*

Japanese cherry blossom is seldom as rich and spectacular as the blossom of many other fruit trees: it is the delicacy and fragility which are prized, not the profusion.

Delicacy and fragility are the hallmarks of most schools of *ikebana*, but they are related to firmer principles. The basis of the art is that any arrangement must show the Leading Principle (Heaven), the Subordinate Principle (Earth), and the Reconciling Principle (Man). Three separate plants or branches may be used to suggest these, or a single branch if one part is trained upwards, a second downwards, and a third bent sideways.

This symbolic rigidity—which sounds so likely to lead to pretentiousness, but which in practice never seems to, since flowers are more simply eloquent than theories—is not applied to plants and flowers outside the discipline of *ikebana*. But the growing and exhibition of *bonsai*—miniature trees and plants—can be seen as another sign of the same impulse, the ordering of nature. In the limited space of many ordinary Japanese gardens, or as the native equivalent of window-boxes where there is no garden at all, *bonsai* are displayed with great pride, and some are handed on from generation to generation as treasured heirlooms. Even the humble cabbage plant is drilled into shapes and colours unknown to it in its usual cultivated form, and the result is that transfiguring of the low and commonplace which appeals so much to the Japanese.

As in the West, flowers are associated with the great family ceremonies of marriage and death. At a wedding feast the pine, bamboo and apricot are brought together because their emblematic qualities are thought appropriate to the occasion, and similarly flowers which easily fall are not used. In the Shinto roadside cemetery, the natural flowers blend with the artificial ones, papered and waxed and offered along with rice, oranges, and even stones. They seem a frail but purposeful echo of the richer carvings at Nikko, where, on the side of a temple, peonies and chrysan-themums are carved and polychromed on a gold background of wood. The lily is gilded, certainly: but no Japanese would think such 'improving' of nature a thing to be regretted at all.

88

PLATE 33 : Korakuen Garden, Tokyo

The Korakuen Garden is in Bunkyo-ku or 'ward', in which many of the leading universities of Tokyo are found, including Tokyo University itself: the area is well named, for *bunka* is 'culture'. But culture is broad: close by the garden is the city's main baseball stadium, 'Velodrome' (for bicycle races), ice-skating rink, and *judo* school.

For those who prefer gentler exercise, the Korakuen Garden is well suited. It is now a public garden, but originally it was the site of Prince Tokugawa of Mito's mansion. Tokugawa Mitsukuni was one of the more enlightened aristocratic leaders of the early Edo Period, and was responsible for the *Dai-Nihon-shi* ('A History of Great Japan'). He was also much open to Chinese influence, and took under his patronage the Chinese expatriate designer, Shu Shun Sui (1600–1682). It was Shu Shun Sui who originally designed the Korakuen Garden, and his calligraphy can be seen in a tablet on the Karamon, or Chinese Gate, which is the entrance to the garden.

PLATE 34: Nimomaru Garden, Imperial Palace, Tokyo

PLATE 35: Senshukaku Garden, Tokushima, Shikoku

Standing in the middle of Tokyo, the Korakuen is the still centre at the heart of the twentieth-century storm. Here are a waterfall of moss, a 'dry' river of stones, a lake, irises, artificial hills, bound and strutted trees, red lacquer bridges. One of the pleasant minor features is the stone bridge, known as the Bridge of the Full Moon, because it is made in a semi-circle, with its reflected image in the water completing the circle. But most of the original buildings constructed by the Tokugawa of Mito family were destroyed in the great Kanto earthquake of 1923, and have not been rebuilt. Among these was the Biidoro-chaya, or Glass Teahouse, so called because glass was used for the windows instead of paper—an indication of how rare this was in pre-Meiji Japan.

Another Tokyo garden, but one not normally open to the public, is that of the Imperial Palace in Chiyoda-ku. This was the Shogun's palace until 1869, when the last of the Shoguns surrendered his authority to the Emperor Meiji. The main buildings were destroyed by bombing during the second world war and have only recently been completed. The Palace is approached over the moat across the Nijubashi, a large double bridge of a design more Palladian than Japanese. The bound trees of the Nimomaru Garden in the palace grounds (bound in straw to protect them after transplanting) are typical of the Japanese blend of utility with beauty, sharing only their plain severity with the still atmosphere of the Senshukaku rock garden, where the water and rock are intended for nothing but contemplation.

PLATE 36: Waterfall, Kenrokuen Park, Kanazawa

The waterfall which descends from the Hisago-ike pond in the Kenrokuen Park is a sharp contrast. Here, in what is accepted as one of the three most beautiful landscape gardens in Japan, the emphasis is on size and movement: *Kenroku* means six features or combinations, these being vastness, solemnity, care in arrangement, age, running water, and charm of scenery. The Kenrokuen is large—twenty-two acres—and is now a public park, though it was originally laid out by a local *daimyo* in the seventeenth century and became the home of the Marquis Maeda. Whereas the Korakuen in Tokyo is all contrived, a deliberately artificial zone of peace in a great city centre, the Kenrokuen is a natural setting on a grand scale—in a sense the Ritsurin of the Japan Sea area. There are, it is true, three artificial hills, but the whole park is intended to be an extension of the landscape that surrounds it. From the larger of the two ponds, Kasumi-ga-ike, the city of Kanazawa can be seen, with Mount Utatsu lying behind, the Japan Sea in the distance, and the mountains of the Noto peninsula stretching across the horizon.

The swift rapids
Are blocked by rocks,
Yet, though the stream
Is sundered, in the end
It unites again.

The Heian Shrine is the supreme example in Japan of reverence for the spirit of the past rather than the things of the past; for its immense buildings, which even to the trained eye seem to be authentically of the Heian period, were in fact completed only in 1895, and the last major reconstruction was just before the second world war. They are a replica of the first Imperial Palace, built in AD 794, and are dedicated to the memory of the Emperor Kammu, the founder of the city of Kyoto.

As the chief Shinto shrine of Kyoto, it follows the Shinto practice of using much bright crimson and multiple roofs and towers. The main buildings are the Otemmon or main gate, the Shinden or main hall, the Daigokuden or great hall of state, the two towers of Soryu-ro and Byakko-ro (the second of which can be seen in the photograph), and the Taihei-Kaku bridge, a roofed bridge which is reflected in the water of the Seiho pond.

Two great festivals are held annually at the shrine, on April 15th and October 22nd. The second is the more important: this is the Jidai Matsuri or 'Festival of Ages', in which a procession moves through the city to the shrine, its members dressed to represent important periods in the history of Kyoto—incorporating such characters as Tomoe-Gozen, a general's wife who dressed as a warrior and fought alongside her husband; Toyotomi Hideyoshi, the sixteenth-century military leader who unified the country; and the triumphal return from his campaigns in the north-east of Sakanoue-no-Tamuramaro.

These military preoccupations are not the concern of the hundreds of *gohei* or paper prayers attached to the twigs of the *sakaki*-tree. These, a typical feature of Shinto shrines, are both prayers and offerings, representing in fact strips of cloth, since cloth was formerly offered (along with food and drink) as spiritual nourishment for the gods living in the shrine. They ask for good fortune, cures of ill-health, children, and safe journeys; and as they are caught in the breeze their white flutterings seem like the blossom of prayer, a logical emotional extension of the Japanese concern with the fragile, enduring cherry.

The Momoyama Period (1573–1615) was a time of much castle and citadel building. Earlier castles had been built in impregnable places and purely as military bases; but in the previous period, the Muromachi, the feudal lords began to use open places for their forts rather than difficult country: this is perhaps some indication of their power, for they used these forts to live in as well as garrison strongholds.

Very few of the original Muromachi or Momoyama castles remain, though many of them—such as those at Osaka, Nagoya, and Hiroshima—are faithful replicas, generally laid over a core of reinforced concrete so as to guard against future fires and earthquakes. Nagoya Castle was completely destroyed in the 1945 bombing, but has since been rebuilt at a cost of 600 million yen, and Osaka Castle was reconstructed in 1931. The gold and splendour of these military mansions was utterly different from the simple temple architecture of the period, but their roof-structure and basic plan was indeed originally based on Zen Buddhist temples.

Himeji Castle, thirty-five miles west of Kobe, contains some of the few extant examples of Momoyama citadel architecture: part of the castle is in fact earlier than the Momoyama period, for the keep, which still stands, was originally built by Akamatsu Sadanori in the fourteenth century. The castle itself is typical with its white walls, high *donjon*, and curved coppery roofs. These white-plastered walls have given it a name which is sometimes used—Hakurojo or 'white heron's castle'. Round it is a moat with stout bastions, the foreground of the photograph here.

> *Ah! The old castle—what does it say?*
> *The ripples by the bank—what do they reply?*
> *Think silently on the age that has gone,*
> *A hundred years even as yesterday.*

From 1192 until 1333 Kamakura, thirty miles south-west of Tokyo, was the capital of Japan, and during this period the *samurai* class grew to be the most important in the country. But it was also the greatest period of realistic technique in sculpture, and is indeed regarded as the golden age of Japanese sculpture. The casting of bronze images was perfected, and the Daibutsu (Great Buddha) of Amida Nyorai at Kamakura is the finest example of this. This huge statue, second only to the Nara Daibutsu in size among ancient Japanese bronzes, is a seated figure, originally enclosed in a temple which was washed away by tidal waves in 1495, since when it has stood in the open.

The Daibutsu was cast in 1252 by Ono Goroemon, considered to be one of the finest sculptors of the Kamakura Period. The slightly bowed head with eyes half-closed is the conventional pose of the Amida Buddha, symbolising unruffled calm and an absence of straining after worldly things. The hands resting on the lap, with the palms uppermost and the thumbs touching, stand for firmness of faith, and the long ear-lobes for omniscience and good fortune. The height of the figure is over forty feet, and a staircase inside leads up as far as the Buddha's shoulders. It was of the similarly hollow Nara Daibutsu that Issa wrote a *haiku* which is characteristic of his sly juxtapositions:

> *Emerging from the nose*
> *Of Great Buddha's statue:*
> *A swallow comes.*

Representations of the Buddha in his various aspects can be found all over Japan, in all sizes and made of all materials: bronze, stone, wood, lacquer and concrete. The commonest are the small stone figures known as *Jizo*, which are placed by the roadside as guardians of travellers' shrines or in the fields as protectors of the crops. Most of these are simple and even crude examples of folk-carving, but they are now also produced in large quantities as souvenirs and are sold through the folk-craft shops of Tokyo and Kyoto. The oddest of all Buddha figures is perhaps the Daibutsu which stands on the Jumonji-Baru plateau near Beppu: it was built in 1927 by a farmer's son who had become a millionaire and who commissioned it in a spirit of repentance for the evils of the world. Made of concrete and bone ashes, it towers twenty-six feet higher than even the Nara Daibutsu.

The Shukkei-en Garden may act as a representation of the endurance not only of Hiroshima but of Japan in general. Built in 1620 by the lord of the district, Asano Nagakira, to be the landscape garden of his villa, it is a typical *tsukiyama* or hill garden, modelled after the scenery of Lake Sei in China. It stands on the banks of the Ota River in the north-east of the city, and escaped the worst ravages of the 1945 bomb. Since the war it has become the most popular public park in Hiroshima, the only substantial link with the past in a place which has been almost entirely reconstructed since 1945. In that year a great city-building programme was started, and now Hiroshima is a completely modern growth, with the scars of war scarcely visible. But one is not allowed thus to escape from a realisation of what happened on August 6th, 1945. The Peace Memorial Park, Hall, Museum, and Cenotaph, the statue of the Children of the Atomic Bomb, the Atomic Dome (formerly the Industrial Promotion Hall, and the only solid building to survive in the centre of the explosion) with its deliberately preserved shell, the Peace Boulevard which runs east to west through the city—all testify that Hiroshima makes sure that no visitor will forget the city's moment of history. For it is a centre of tourism as well as of industry, with over 50,000 foreign tourists a year: a gruesome fact.

Hara Tamiki was a poet of Hiroshima who experienced the explosion at first hand, and who committed suicide in 1951 after doctors had confirmed that he had the symptoms of radiation disease. In a novel, *Summer Flowers*, and in poems such as 'In the fire', he celebrated the same power of regeneration embodied in the Shukkei-en Garden:

> *In the fire, a telegraph pole*
> *At the heart of the fire.*
> *A telegraph pole like a stamen,*
> *Like a candle,*
> *Blazing up, like a molten*
> *Red stamen.*
> *In the heart of the fire on the other bank*
> *From this morning, one by one,*
> *Fear has screamed*
> *Through men's eyes. At the heart of the fire*
> *A telegraph pole, like a stamen.*

Custom and Ceremony: The Gesture of a People

PLATE 41: War-veteran
at Shikinen-sengu ceremony,
Jingu Shrine, Ise-shima

'Custom and ceremony', much as Yeats celebrated them in his poem 'A Prayer for
my Daughter', are threads which run through the whole of Japanese life. The year
is studded with traditional observances, rituals, and festivals, the greatest of them
being Ganjitsu, New Year, when the first three (and sometimes the first five) days
of January are set aside and work stops everywhere. The entrances of houses are
decorated with pairs of pine trees to which bamboo-stems are tied. Above the
entrance is hung the *shimenawa*, a rope with tufts of straw and strips of white paper,
among which are hung fern leaves, an orange, and a small lobster: the fern suggesting the expansion of good fortune throughout the new year; the lobster, with
its bent back, carries the wish that the inhabitants may live until they are bent with
age, and therefore signifies longevity; and the orange represents the continuity of
life, because *daidai* means not only 'orange' but 'from generation to generation'—

the type of happy pun which the Japanese love to make. Kites are flown, ornamental battledores are exchanged and briefly played with, until they are shut away for another year with the ceremonial dolls. Families sit round playing *hyakunin-isshu*, 'single songs of a hundred poets', a version of snap in which someone reads the first half of a poem from this thirteenth-century anthology while the players choose an appropriate card from the hundred cards containing the second halves of the poems spread out on the floor. *O-mochi*, sweet and glutinous rice-cakes, are eaten, and a variety of foods with auspiciously punning names: *kazunoko*, herring-roe, which also means 'many children', *mamé*, black beans and 'robust', and *kachiguri* (chestnuts), because *kachi* means 'victory'.

There is the Hina-Matsuri (Dolls' Festival) on March 3rd and the Kodomono-hi (Children's or Boys' Festival) on May 5th. Another children's day is November 15th, the Shichi-Go-San, which means 'Seven-Five-Three': on this day children of these ages are taken to their local Shinto shrines by their parents, and prayers are offered in thanks for protection and for guidance in the future.

The chief festival of the summer is the Tanabata-matsuri, the star festival, which celebrates the coming together of the Gemini. This day, in July or August, is particularly noted in Sendai, when the streets are decorated with bamboo branches hung with paper streamers and prayers, together with paper and papier mâché shapes of a size and grotesqueness reminding one of Mardi Gras festivals elsewhere.

Each temple and shrine has its own annual festival, and so do most towns and villages. In them, history and mythology blend. But the most deeply embedded of all festivals is Bon, held in July, which is a symbolic reunion with the spirits of one's ancestors—a kind of All Souls' Day—when cemeteries are visited at night and lanterns are lit in them, in areas with open water illuminated floats and boats are launched, and in the country Bon dances are performed, celebrated in many folk lyrics; for Bon is thought of as a time when not only the spirits of the dead return to the living but also when young men and women are paired off:

> *If you dance this dance,*
> *Better dance it well.*
> *Those who dance it best, they say,*
> *Are better bets for brides.*

The Jingu Shrine at Ise-shima is made of plain unvarnished wood from the *hinoki* (Japanese cypress) found in the forests of the Kiso mountains. Once every twenty years various parts of the shrine are completely razed and new wood is brought in to rebuild them on adjacent plots which are reserved for the purpose. The new parts are rededicated, and new sacred treasures and garments—exact replicas of the old—are made to be kept in them. This rebuilding and rededication is called Shikinen-Sengu.

The photograph shows part of the ceremonial of the 1965 Shikinen-Sengu, when three sacred logs were brought along the river as cross-beams for the Inner Shrine, Kotaijingu, an inner sanctum which is normally not visited by laymen. The logs are brought along the Isuzu River by specially-chosen volunteers led by Shinto priests. The Isuzu has its source within the grounds of the Inner Shrine and flows into the Gulf of Ise—a distance of only about twelve miles, but this short stretch of water is known everywhere in Japan not only for its reputed purity but also for its sacredness. The custom is for all pilgrims to the shrine to rinse their hands and mouths with water from the river before going on to worship.

A kind of holy cannibalism is a feature of the Shikinen-Sengu, by which, for example, the Uji bridge of the Isuzu River is rebuilt. The upper parts of the bridge, also made of *hinoki*, are replaced in the twenty-year cycle by taking the largest supporting pillars from the Inner and Outer Shrines and using these for constructing the torii at each end: traditionally the torii at the outer end of the bridge is made from the Outer Shrine and that at the inner end from the Inner Shrine. So the Jingu Shrines, among the holiest centres of Shinto, are self-perpetuating, part of an endless process of rebirth and regeneration.

PLATE 43: Crowd at Nikko
during May 17th Festival

The main event of the chief Nikko festival each May 17th is the *sennin-gyoretsu* (the thousand-person procession), a parade similar to the Jidai Matsuri at Kyoto: all participants are dressed as priests, *samurai* and so on of the Tokugawa era. In the morning the spirits of Ieyasu, Hideyoshi and Yoritomo are transferred to *mikoshi* (portable shrines), which are then taken in procession to the Otabisho, or Hall of Sojourn. Here *bugaku* music is played and a sacred dance, called Azuma-asobi Suruga-mai, is performed. Then the *mikoshi* are taken back to the Mikoshi-gura, a sacred storehouse specially made for them.

But *mikoshi* are not confined to Nikko alone. All over Japan they can be seen on holy days and at local shrine festivals, often carried along by troupes of young men stripped to loin-cloths and headbands. The men sway and sing under the great weight of their load, and sometimes strengthen and inflame themselves with *saké* before taking it up. All traffic stops as the glittering palanquin, like an Ark of the Lord, is carried by.

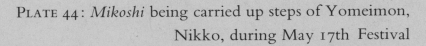

PLATE 44: *Mikoshi* being carried up steps of Yomeimon,
Nikko, during May 17th Festival

In the world of custom and ceremony, Japan is a country of what might be called the male mysteries. At puberty, a Japanese boy must begin to learn that he is a special person, a creature set apart, with responsibilities, skills, and disciplines to be learned. In their different ways the four pictures of adults show this: the hallowed postures and attitudes of *sumo* and *judo*, the set, forbidding face of an imperial servant, the almost balletic grace of the man who has learned to use his knife with the same delicacy and fineness that a *samurai* brought to his sword.

'The value of *sumo*', it has been said, 'lies in its uselessness': a typically Japanese paradox. This 'wrestling done to please the gods' is traditionally traced back to 23 BC, to a match between Taima-no-Kehaya and Nomi-no-Sukune. Kehaya was known as a menace and a bully, and the Emperor summoned the strong men of Japan to defeat him. At this time kicking was permitted in *sumo*, and Sukune, who answered the Emperor's challenge, succeeded in killing the bully with a tremendous kick. Although his methods were unorthodox, Sukune (or Nomi, as he is sometimes called) is considered to be the patron saint of *sumo*.

In *sumo* the participants are naked except for the *mawashi*, a white loin-cloth, and their hair is arranged in traditional *samurai* fashion. The performance itself is framed in ritual—the sprinkling of salt, the cleansing of the mouth with water, the lumbering preliminaries as the wrestlers strike their knees with the palms of their hands and sway from side to side. It is a pure trial of brute strength aided by acquired skill, in which weight is important: a *sumo* player often weighs up to twenty-five stone. The issue is decided when any part of a player's body except his feet touches the ground, or when he steps or is pushed out of the fifteen-foot ring. *Sumo* is today largely a professional sport, watched on television as well as in *sumo* halls, but there are also many student clubs.

Unlike *sumo*, *judo* has spread all over the world. It was systematised less than a hundred years ago, when many conflicting *judo* schools were reconciled, and is now a popular amateur sport. Here strength is much less important than skill; or rather, the emphasis is on using one's *opponent's* strength to one's own advantage. *Judo* is more naturally suited to the generally small, lithe physique of the Japanese than is *sumo*, which requires prodigious—and expensive—eating to reach the required bulk and weight.

Karate (strengthening, and boxing with, the flat of the hand), and *kendo* (fighting with a huge wooden sword), are other native Japanese sports; but the most popular sport of all is the imported baseball, which is eagerly followed in both professional and student teams. The equivalent of the Oxford–Cambridge boat race is the

PLATE 45: *Sumo* wrestlers

PLATE 46: *Judo* wrestlers

PLATE 47: Imperial motor-cycle escort

PLATE 48: Fish-slicer, Tokyo fish-market

annual baseball match between the two leading private universities in Tokyo, Waseda and Keio, which is supported by thousands of people who have no connection with either university. Japanese athletes have also distinguished themselves as Marathon runners, flyweight and bantamweight boxers, freestyle wrestlers, gymnasts, and table-tennis players. But the sport which has made the most spectacular and unlikely progress since the second world war is golf, which in Japan as much as anywhere had become a desirable adjunct of the businessman. With suitable ground for golf courses at a premium, it is an expensive hobby. One of the few substantial patches of green on the grim drive from Tokyo to Yokohama is a golf course, and Japanese businessmen abroad are today as known for their sets of golf-clubs as they used to be for their cameras. As in every other sport they adopt, they play with great seriousness, determination, and skill.

Among all physical cults, however, the most characteristically Japanese is that of bathing. Bathing in Japan is not just a way of getting clean, it is a sensuous ritual, and some of the most popular hotels and inns are those with the finest and most elaborate bathing facilities. The *on-sen* (hot springs) of such places as Atami, Ito and Beppu are holiday places all the year round, and there are few pleasures to equal lying in a steaming hot bath in the open air in December or January, looking out over mountains, a river or the sea, with the air keen, cold, and clear. Mixed public bathing is now uncommon, but it is still usual to bathe naked with one's own sex in such inns. Here is a place for relaxation and gossip, with the utilitarian business of getting clean a necessary but unimportant preliminary. Here, in an atmosphere more like that of the great bathing establishments of ancient Rome than anything else that can be found today, is another aspect of the male mystery, the exclusiveness and *camaraderie* of the male—though in more dubious inns other tastes are catered for, and the maid who offers towel and massage may be expecting more than her words suggest. Governments have repeatedly tried to break down the *on-sen*/brothel syndrome, but perhaps half-heartedly and certainly without much success.

Like their menfolk who bring the sacred logs up the Isuzu River to the shrine, the women who dance the ancient dance known as the *Ise-ondo* through the streets of Ise at the time of Shikinen-Sengu are also chosen volunteers. As in many of the world's cultures, women in Japan are traditionally seen as having their own place and functions and they are jealously kept within these bounds. The common word for 'wife' is still *oku-san*—the person in the inner room—yet on the other hand there has never been any attempt to keep women in quite the almost prison-like seclusion or purdah of some Hindu or Muslim societies. Among the workers, women toil in public along with men, whether planting or harvesting rice, road-mending, caring for the public gardens, street-sweeping, or sometimes even doing heavy manual work. There are more exotic jobs, too, such as the women pearl divers of Toba, not far from Ise, who dive almost naked into the sea to recover the pearl-bearing oysters for the Mikimoto pearl farms.

As in the West, a degree of emancipation has meant that women have found their way into politics, journalism and commerce, as well as carrying out their accustomed role as entertainers (particularly *geisha*) in new ways, such as film stars and pop singers. The traditional theatre of Noh and Kabuki has not allowed them to be performers, and in these dramas female characters are still played by *onnagata* (impersonators). Women have formed their own institutes and clubs, with lecture programmes, home hints, and sightseeing expeditions; and wedding ceremonies are beginning to incorporate notions of costume and performance from abroad. Thus in and near the Gishiki-den or Ceremonial Hall of the Heian Shrine in Kyoto—a favourite place for weddings—one can quite often see a modern western wedding-dress in white juxtaposed with the traditional costume.

Traditionally, a bride comes under the control not only of her husband but also of her mother-in-law, and this has meant—and still means—a hard life for the young woman. But it is noticeable that many households are dominated by the grandmother, who, with the Japanese deference to age, is allowed much power. Women, after years of being suppressed in the families which they have joined through marriage, usually do their own suppressing when their time comes, and meek, self-effacing middle-aged women turn into matriarchs who say what they think and do what they like.

It is still difficult, but not now uncommon, for girls to win their way through to higher education, whether in purely female universities, such as Tokyo Joshi-dai and Tsuda, or in competition with men at any other. As graduates, their future shares the hazards and humiliations common to educated women in most areas of the world. The impetus of the system is to drive all women into early marriage, short-term work (nowadays often as skilled assemblers of transistor parts), or the peripheries of entertainment—bar-hostesses, *maiko*, and beyond that the world of the *pan-pan*, the prostitute, about whom the living poet Kaneko Mitsuharu wrote his cynical poem, 'Song of the tart', which ends:

She yawns, fit
To swallow a man whole.
Never in Japan a crater
As gaping as this yawn.

Wordy, tedious debates,
War-guilt, liberalism,
All these flung into the abyss
Of that tart's yawn
Make only a ripple.

116

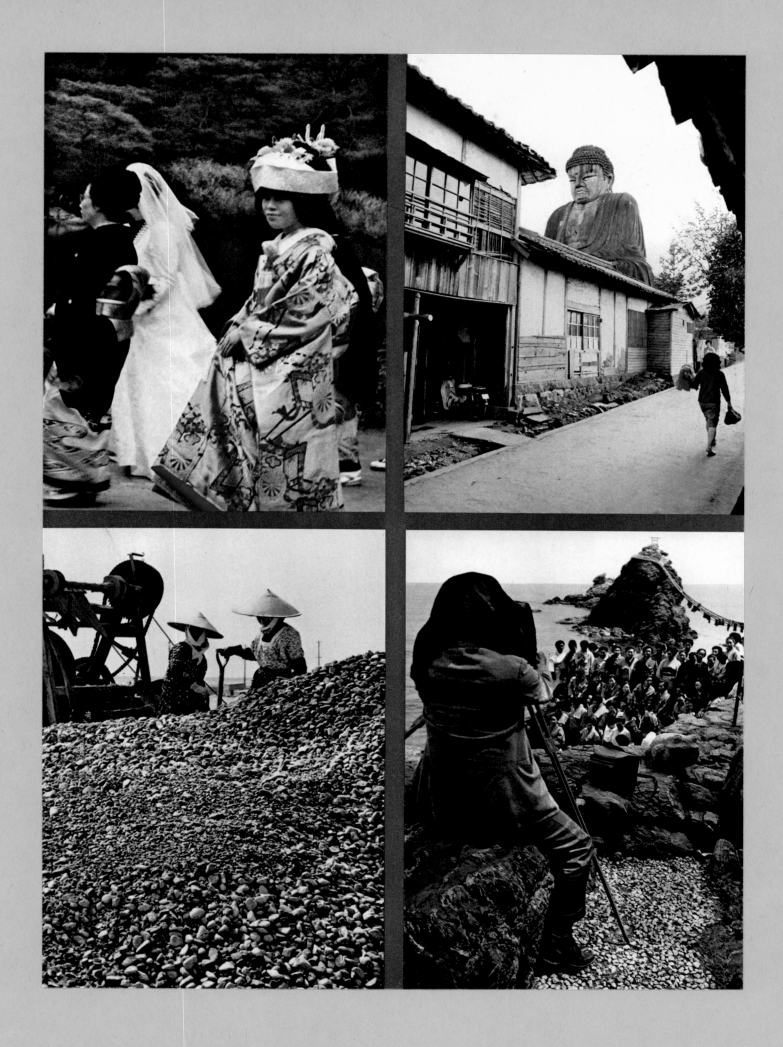

The face of both Japanese religion and Japanese art can be seen as a mask rather than a likeness, an intermediary deliberately placed between the spirit of the object and the spectator of the object. It was this hieratic remoteness that so attracted Yeats towards Japanese art and drama, but it must also be said that it is something that repels many non-Japanese. Whether in art, religion, or ordinary life, the grotesque or the inscrutable present a challenge to one's accepted notions of 'taking things at their face value'. The huge wooden figure of a Nio, such as Kongo-Rikishi, the guardian-figure often found in the gateways of Buddhist temples, with his fierce scowl and baleful eyes, may seem the product of some inhuman malevolent impulse rather than showing the 'incomparable vigour and animation' to which the guide-book directs one.

Shinto and Buddhism abound in images, both benign and grotesque, but Zen Buddhism withdraws importance from the image and concentrates it on 'the Buddha within': so that the face of the contemplative Zen priest itself becomes an image, a mask covering the utterly still, world-ignoring soul. In art, the representation of this can be seen in the face of the Daibutsu in the Shohoji Temple at Gifu, very different from many embodyings of the Buddha both in appearance and method of construction; for this is not made of bronze (like those at Kamakura or Nara), nor of wood, which is a common material for religious sculpture in Japan, but of basket-work, to which paper covered with *sutras* (Buddhist texts) have been pasted, and the whole surface then finished in lacquer. This odd kind of sculptural *collage* is effective, and the use of lacquer interestingly underlines the value of this material in Japanese art and objects: it preserves and decorates humbler stuff—in particular, wood—and in a country with few mineral resources but plenty of trees this is important. Japanese lacquer is itself the product of a tree, and was an early export, both in the form of a technique taught to visiting Chinese craftsmen as early as the mid-fifteenth century and also in goods sent abroad. Hence the 'japanned boxes' of our ancestors.

If the Shohoji Daibutsu signifies the mask of calm, the Nio and the 'devil masks' of popular festivals show the Medusa image, the compression of evil into concrete form so as to repel evil. This distancing can be seen too in the masks of evil characters in the Noh and Kabuki drama; and in the same way the masks of the 'good' characters seem to be paradigms or essences of goodness. For traditional Japanese drama is firmly etched in terms of black and white, so that in the famous tale of the forty-seven *ronin* (itself the theme of a popular Kabuki play, *Chushingura*), for example, the motives and actions of the loyal retainers, who avenged the death of their lord by murdering his enemy and then committed suicide, is seen without any of the subtler shading of western tragedy. Such plays are, in fact, at the stage of development of the 'revenge' play in England when Shakespeare adopted and transformed the convention. Thus the mask can mean an avoidance of subtlety, a concentration on the clear-cut 'meaning' of men's motives and actions. Here the function is different from the basically utilitarian but also somehow emblematic mask of the *kendo* player, secure behind his protective bars yet more sinister than the familiar fencer and bee-keeper who are, after all, similarly equipped. It is, perhaps, another aspect of the Japanese 'male mystery', an exclusiveness, a distancing that keeps the world at arm's length—quite literally, in the case of the *kendo* player.

PLATE 57: Zen priest, Daisen-in, Daitokuji Temple, Kyoto

PLATE 58:
Daibutsu, Shohoji Temple, Gifu

PLATE 59:
Ko-omote (female mask),
Noh theatre, Tokyo

PLATE 60:
Doll of one of 47 Ronin,
Sengakuji Temple, Tokyo

PLATE 61:
Kendo player, University of Tokyo

PLATE 62:
Devil mask, Asakusa, Tokyo

The mask may also be a mirror of Japan, reflecting—as it is meant to do in a Shinto shrine—the unseen gods: a blank which reveals whatever one wants it to reveal. In this setting each object is a token of the gods: the lacquer pillars, the guardian *koma-inu*, the jars of rice and *saké*, the priest himself immobile before the scriptures, even the floor which itself acts as a mirror. The rites of religion and the rituals of Japanese behaviour are formal masks which have been adopted to stabilise the violence and potential chaos of a malevolent world, seen in earthquakes, typhoons, tidal waves, fires and floods. A traditional Japanese sentiment is the desire for permanence in an impermanent and shifting world, as expressed by the eight-century AD poet of the Manyoshu, Yamanoue Okura:

> *We are helpless in this world.*
> *The years and months slip past*
> *Like a swift stream, which grasps and drags us down.*
> *A hundred pains pursue us, one by one . . .*
> *We grudge life moving on*
> *But we have no redress.*
> *I would become as those*
> *Firm rocks that see no change.*
> *But I am a man in time*
> *And time must have no stop.*

So the mask establishes something permanent, gives continuity, as an heirloom or inheritance, linking past and present. Through it, as through the actor's *persona*, the past speaks. Here is the ideal at which Yeats unsuccessfully aimed, for he was part of a society in which masks are only for clowns and children.

Japan has been called, by travel-writers and journalists, 'the paradise of children', and however much one's gorge may rise at the thought thus expressed, there is some truth in it. From birth until puberty, Japanese children are coddled, indulged, petted, praised and made much of in a far more extravagant way than children elsewhere. In a country of present-giving, presents are loaded on them. They travel at reduced fares but are allowed to take up as much room in buses, trams and trains as they like, and if there is standing room only it is the adults who stand, not the children.

All this might lead one to suppose that Japanese children would behave in a shockingly spoiled way; but in public, at any rate, what is much more apparent is their liveliness and alertness rather than their tempers and tantrums. They are very close physically to their parents, being breast-fed commonly until two or even three—or at least being allowed comfort at the mother's nipple—and for several years they are carried round on the mother's back in the padded extension of the *kimono*; yet though this seems to encourage a contentedness which looks dangerously like complete passivity, their physical and mental progress is not stunted. At an early age in school they are faced with the rudiments of *kanji* (Chinese ideograms), and learn to handle an ink-brush at a stage when other children are painfully mastering the grip on a pencil. In their group behaviour—and everywhere one sees children on school expeditions to parks, temples, museums and sightseeing spots— they are as disciplined and cohesive as Japanese always are in such circumstances.

In the cycle of the Japanese year, they are at the centre of most festivals, from the Hina-matsuri and the Kodomono-hi to the Shichi-go-san. In the Kabuki theatre, the warmest tears and murmurs are for the child-actor, almost certainly one of a long line of professional actors, who flutes his words in a peculiarly stylised way as he resolves to avenge his father—a favourite turn of plot.

But it ought to be made clear that all this is much truer of the small boy than of the small girl, for Japan is, after all, a man's country. The supposedly self-effacing virtues thought proper to women in such a context are bred into girls at an early age, and the progress from girl to woman is, one supposes, thereby made the smoother. For boys it is different, and it is here that tensions arise. The change from primary to secondary school at the age of twelve marks an even greater step in social adjustment than it does elsewhere, and though more liberal notions of

education have spread since the war (partly influenced by the immediate post-war reforms put forward by the American educational commission and made law in 1947), the older practices are still apparent. The stress in many secondary schools on hard academic grind (the teacher is the provider of facts which must be learned by rote and drilled) and tough physical fitness reminds one of the less progressive type of British public school, and indeed there have been several post-war experiments in bringing specifically this type of boarding-school education into Japan—outside the state system, of course.

Students in Japan, from kindergarten right through to the end of their university days, are commonly uniformed, from the charmingly doll-like clothes of the private kindergartens to the German-inspired black uniforms of secondary-school and university students, with their peaked caps, high collars, and identifying badges on cap and collar. Girls wear sailor-suits, attractive enough for ten-year-olds but lumpishly unbecoming when worn by solid young women of nineteen or twenty, as they often are.

Worldly sophistication is not welcomed in young people, and in the nineteen-fifties there was a good deal of shocked comment in the newspapers and elsewhere about the supposed emergence of a new breed, the *taiyo-no-zoku* or 'children of the sun': rebellious teenagers, usually of well-off parents, who circulated in gangs to drink, smoke, drive fast sports cars and motor-bicycles, and have promiscuous sex. Or so one would gather from the films and novels about them, the most famous example being a novel by Shintaro Ishihara, itself called *Taiyo-no-zoku*, which rather surprisingly won the Akutagawa Prize, one of the top literary awards. But no doubt there has been more talk than substance about the phenomenon. Rebelliousness and heterodoxy are not common among even Japanese adolescents (the followers of Zengakuren, the student union, have their own brand of orthodox activism), and Kaneko Mitsuharu's poem 'Opposition' seems to strike an uncharacteristic attitude:

> In my youth I was opposed to school.
> And now, again,
> I'm opposed to work . . .
> Of course I'm opposed to 'the Japanese spirit'
> And duty and human feeling make me vomit.
> I'm against any government anywhere
> And show my bum to authors' and artists' circles . . .

Far from being 'the age-old cry of adolescent insurrection' (as one English critic has commented), it may rather be taken as the almost wistful protest of middle-age watching from the sidelines the antics of the *mobo* and *moga* (slang terms for 'modern boy' and 'modern girl') and becoming inflamed at the sight. The decorous crocodiles of schoolchildren are more typical even of post-war Japan.

128

PLATE 65: Child at Ritsurin Park, Takamatsu, Shikoku

PLATE 66: Schoolchildren on expedition, Lake Biwa

PLATE 70: Kyoto Tower   PLATE 71: *Pachinko* parlour, Tokyo

Japan has been a pioneer in the development of colour television. There are also over forty commercial radio and television networks, the so-called Tokyo Tower and Kyoto Tower being transmitters for two of them. Tokyo Tower belongs to the Nippon Television City Corporation; it is well over a thousand feet high, and indeed is said to be the highest of its kind in the world. It has two observation platforms and a five-storey Modern Science Museum at its base.

Modern Tokyo has its less spectacular modernisms. The side streets and alleys off the main roads, here as elsewhere in urban Japan, are full of bars, cafes, restaurants, and *pachinko* parlours: *pachinko* is an automatic-game machine, in which a coin releases a ball that can be spun round a wheel, and if it enters an appropriate hole a prize is won. The craze hit Japan long before Bingo hit Britain, and it still survives, having a similar insidious hold on its devotees. Without the other distractions of a lottery or a pools system, many Japanese put long hours of mindless activity into manipulating *pachinko* machines. New parlours are started frequently, and that shown in the photograph here is a new one, marked as such by the display of elaborate artificial flowers, the sign by which one may recognise any new shop in Japan.

132

Tokyo has a character of its own, certainly: the inhabitant of Tokyo is reputed to have an up-to-date sophistication, as distinct from the smooth old-world charm (or, it has been said, oiliness) of the Kyoto man or the hard-headed commercial acumen of the Osaka man. But, as in most great cities, it is a character that splits up into the separate atmospheres of different districts, from the narrow alleys of Shinjuku and Asakusa (the Montmartre and Plaka of Tokyo) to the broad boulevards and public buildings of Chiyoda-ku, and from the warren of second-hand book-shops in Kanda and the antique and curio shops of Roppongi to the darker, meaner districts east of the Sumida River, crossed by over fifteen bridges as it flows into Tokyo Harbour.

PLATE 72: Part of Olympic Stadium, Tokyo

PLATE 73: Tokyo Tower

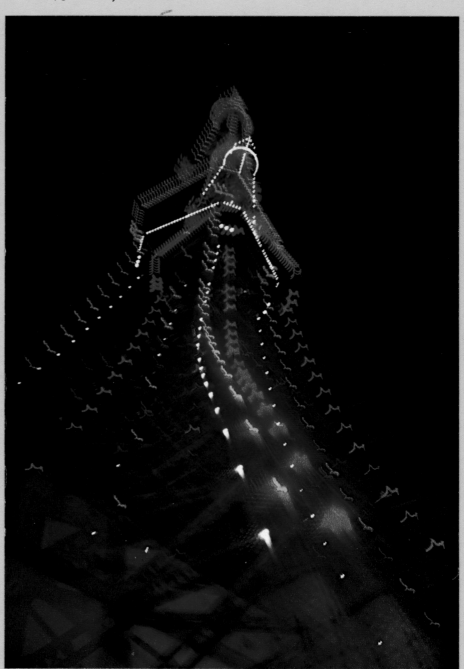

The prevalence of natural good taste in Japan should not make anyone imagine that there is not also an abundance of the bizarre, the grotesque, and the vulgar. The grotesqueness of some religious images has already been noted: the secular world has its share too. Sometimes it is a matter of juxtapositions, as in the *ikebana* which forms a climbing-frame for a captive monkey, a piece of dubious whimsy which could be seen as a comment—probably unintended—on the Ikenobo school of *ikebana*, in its framework of stiff artificiality; animated by an entirely unsuitable creature. The plastic deer sold as souvenirs at Nara seem like irreverent Disney-like caricatures of the numerous real deer (over 150 of them) which wander through Nara Park, traditionally regarded as divine messengers; yet undoubtedly they are simply practical commercial products, as well as being an indication of the frequent uncertainty of Japanese taste when confronted with alien models. It was this shrewd vulgarity of spirit that the modern poet Takenaka Iku has satirised in his 'Tourist Japan':

> *Fujiyama—we sell.*
> *Miyajima—we sell.*
> *Nikko—we sell.*
> *Japan—we sell anywhere.*
> *Naruto, Aso—*
> *We sell it all.*
> *Prease, prease, come and view!*
> *Me rub hands,*
> *Put on smile.*
> *Money, money—that's the thing . . .*

(The original is written in a deliberately pidgin Japanese corresponding to this English version.)

Some of the bizarreness of Japan is only a matter of plain unfamiliarity: and this is particularly true of food, everywhere notoriously parochial in its appeal. The slabs of dried fish, the live octopuses in fishmongers' tanks, the crucified squid drying in the sun—these are no stranger to a Japanese than snails and frogs' legs are popularly supposed to be to a Frenchman or haggis to a Scot. A Japanese banquet—and the Japanese are fond of celebratory eating—is intended to be, like all Japanese food, 'a feast for the eyes', and for some westerners this aesthetic appeal is never transferred to the palate. But even for those who never acquire a taste for peculiarly Japanese dishes, there are some—such as *sukiyaki* (sliced beef and vegetables cooked in a pan over a brazier) and *tempura* (fish and vegetables cooked in vegetable oil after being dipped in batter)—which make no demands on foreign forebearance. Japanese food tends to emphasise the natural taste of the ingredients, though perhaps the most characteristic flavour is that of *shoyu* (soya sauce), which is the usual accompaniment to rice, vegetables, meat and fish.

134

PLATE 78: After a banquet, Himeji

The world of business and the world of pleasure unite in the *geisha* party, in which badinage, silly songs and silly stories conspire with food and *saké* to oil the wheels of affairs. The American servicemen who, immediately after the war, are reported to have ranged hungrily down the Ginza in Tokyo yelling, 'We want geesha!' were on the wrong track. The *geisha* is primarily an entertainer provided for on business expenses: the nearest equivalent in the western world might be the much-publicised American 'Bunny', for as far as the ordinary guest (or customer) is concerned, both *geisha* and 'Bunnies' are equally untouchable. In their appearance and behaviour, *geisha* have probably adapted less to modern life than many things in Japan, but they are often fully up to date in their knowledge of what is going on in the world—or at least in the world as it comes to them in the form of company directors, politicians, journalists and the like. In a country of big circulation newspapers, *geisha* have an ear for gossip and scandal, and one of their strictest jobs must be to know when to keep silent and when to talk. But to most Japanese men they are either an unthinkable luxury or an anachronistic embarrassment. They are among the decorative fossils of Japan.

136

PLATE 79: Newspaper
office, Nagoya

PLATE 80: *Geisha* party,
Himeji

Mount Fuji (properly expressed as Fuji-san or Fuji, never as Fujiyama, a western solecism) is the highest, holiest, and most celebrated mountain in Japan. It is also a volcano, but not an active one, though the faint wisps of steam that sometimes wreathe its summit indicate that it is dormant rather than dead. The last eruption was in 1707, when Edo (Tokyo), seventy-five miles away, was covered with a six-inch layer of ashes.

Painters, poets, pilgrims and lovers have made it famous. One of the best-known series by Hokusai is his *Fuji Hyakkei* or 'The Hundred Views of Fuji', in which he recorded aspects of the mountain from different viewpoints and at different seasons; for one of the things that has made Fuji a challenge to all those who want to record it (including photographers) is the variety of faces it can show.

Sometimes it cannot be seen at all, and Bashō notes even this as significant:

> *And pleasant, too,*
> *Not to see Fuji*
> *For thick mist and rain.*

Thus the momentary withdrawing of the perfect mountain means that it will be the better appreciated when it is revealed once again.

It also acts as a scale to which other things are related, as in Buson's

> *Fuji alone*
> *Left unburied*
> *By young green leaves.*

Or Issa's

> *Slowly, slowly, climb*
> *Up and up Mount Fuji,*
> *O snail.*

And its influence is felt as stretching far beyond its immediate setting, as in Bashō's

> *What I brought home*
> *From Edo was a fan*
> *Cooled by Fuji's breeze.*

Pilgrims climb it to make their devotions at the Sengen Shrine near its summit, and since 1860 (when the first British Minister, Sir Rutherford Alcock, made the ascent) it has also been the goal of visiting foreigners, who thereby feel that they have 'done' Japan in proper fashion. But until the Meiji Restoration it was forbidden to women, though—characteristically—the wife of another British Minister managed to break this ban. Now it makes a favourite expedition for student groups, and is still the occasional setting for love-suicides. It is a shrine, a decorative emblem, a nation's focal point of patriotic emotions, and a mystery. Unlike Basho, a traveller who passes near it without seeing it may well feel cheated, for among all the symbols of Japan it suggests most strongly the heart of the country—nature beautiful in its potential violence, and man struggling to express it.

Images of Permanence

The Emperor Meiji once wrote a wistful *tanka* on the reconciliation he hoped to see between the old Japan and the new ideas and inventions he saw flooding into his country in the late nineteenth century:

> *In my garden*
> *Side by side*
> *Native plants, foreign plants,*
> *Growing together.*

It is typical that the image he chose for this reconciliation was plants in a garden, for the Japanese have developed the cultivation and crossing of flowers and plants and the development of gardens in a way unequalled by any other race. That hoary old anthology-piece by T. E. Brown about a garden being 'a lovesome thing, God wot' sounds like a fulsome nineteenth-century translation of a *tanka* (though of course it is not), and indeed horticulturalists and landscape-gardeners all over the world have reason to be grateful to the Japanese. And not only these, for the

140

Emperor's wish to see native and foreign blending together in Japan has taken another turn: Japan itself has begun to influence those foreigners who have come into contact with it, in a variety of ways, from bamboo- and felt-tipped pens to a Kabuki-based production of *King Lear*, and from the shapes and glazes of pottery to transplantings of *haiku*. The teachings of Japanese Zen and the films of Ozu are fashionable in the West, and the sight of postcards of Hokusai and Hiroshige has become as common as those of Van Gogh and Cézanne.

But behind this rediscovery of Japan by the West, behind the hectic competitive modernisation, lies a country and a people still isolated by nature and custom in their own way of life. They have come to terms with the twentieth-century world, but much still exists in a continuity that was already old when Minamoto Sanetomo, who died in the early thirteenth century, wrote

That it might be so always,
This world of ours—
These tiny fisherboats
Rowed close to the beach . . .
Splendid to see!

PLATE 83: Fishing boats off Maizuru, Japan Sea

PLATE 84: 'Green Hell', Beppu

PLATE 85:
Inner Garden, Meiji Shrine, Tokyo

Water like smoke
Hanging above stones
In the mists of autumn.

Motionless after rain
The groves that lead
To the iris garden.

The route from Nikko to Lake Chuzenji passes close to the Kegon Waterfall, which falls 330 feet in a sheer drop from the edge of a gorge to a huge deep basin below. It is a favourite place for love-suicides. The whole of this area is noted for its water-falls, many of them having fanciful descriptive names, such as Kirifuri-no-taki ('mist-falling cascade'), Shirakumo ('white cloud'), Shiraito-no-taki ('white threads cascade'), and even Somen-daki ('vermicelli cascade'), so called because of an imagined resemblance between the threads of falling water and the strings of a variety of Japanese pasta. Nearby is Sake-no-izumi, or 'the *saké* spring', because formerly the water that bubbled up there was supposed to taste like *saké*.

Water, indeed, is a liquid for connoisseurs in Japan, both as a drink and aesthetically. Like the Arabs, the Japanese have a whole vocabulary to devote to it, and the sight of it in motion or repose, the many different sounds of it, are celebrated in poems. The most famous *haiku* of all is a complex aural apprehension of water: Bashō's

> *An old pond:*
> *A frog jumps in—*
> *Sound of water.*

And a *senryu* implicitly praises the water of a particular place:

> *If it could be wrapped*
> *Water would make a fine*
> *Present from Kyoto.*

As early as the poems of the *Manyoshu*, water was seen with sensuous vitality, the accompaniment of growth and fertility:

> *The spring has come, the spring*
> *That wakens the fern's buds*
> *Above the waterfall*
> *That wets the rocks with spray.*

In all its moods—flowing, agitated, mysterious (as in the steaming pools of Beppu), swollen and placid after rain (as in the lake of the Meiji Shrine's Inner Garden), or frozen and almost completely arrested, as here at the Kegon Waterfall—water is the most often evoked and highest praised of the four elements.

144

The sky becomes water,
The water becomes sky—
Looked at upside down.

The bridge is so long
That as I wave goodbye
At the far end,
I cannot see your face:
Only your lifted sleeve.

PLATE 88: Setabashi,
Lake Biwa

Amanohashidate is a sand-bar two miles long and about 200 feet wide, stretching across the Bay of Miyazu and thus forming a natural bridge with the sea on one side and the lagoon of Aso-Umi on the other. This 'Bridge of Heaven'—the literal meaning of the name—is another of Hayashi Razan's 'Scenic Trio' and has, too, the curious mythological reputation of being the place on which Izanagi and Izanami stood as they embraced one another in the monumental act of love of which the islands of Japan were the result. Along Amanohashidate grow pine trees which have been twisted and bent by the wind. Traditionally—and with a touch of quirkiness—the best view of the scene is had by standing on the slopes of Mount Nariai and looking at it from between one's legs, so that the bridge seems suspended in mid-air; postcards and figurines showing this ungainly stance are bought as souvenirs.

In a country where much water has to be negotiated, bridges have a special importance. *Bashi* (or *hashi*), the Japanese word for bridge, is one of the commonest suffixes in place-names and surnames. Setabashi, which crosses Lake Biwa at its southern tip, is in fact two long bridges joined by a small island. The lake is called Biwa because it is supposed to look like the musical instrument, a curved object resembling a mandolin or a balalaika. There are hills and mountains all round it, and these are the setting for the classical 'Eight Views', consciously selected view-points with poetic associations which are favourite subjects for painters: the evening snow on Mount Hira, the flight of the wild geese at Katata, night rain at Karasaki, the evening bell at Miidera Temple (noted in Bashō's *haiku*:

> *Seven sights were veiled*
> *In mist—then I heard*
> *Mii Temple's bell*),

sunshine and breeze at Awazu, the glow of evening at Seta, the autumn moon at Ishiyama, and sailing boats returning to Yabase.

148

This mountainous district brings out the strong contrast found in Japan between hill and valley—a contrast between the wild and the cultivated, for the slopes of mountains are seldom used by farmers and it is rare to find buildings (even castles) on crags or mountain-tops; whereas the valleys and plains are turned into intensively cultivated gardens, the farmhouses and outbuildings themselves existing in a garden setting. The farmhouses are thickly thatched, sometimes single-storeyed buildings as is usual in Japanese town houses, but often—as in the Takayama district —with two or even three storeys. The thatch keeps them cool in summer and warm in winter, and round them are substantial hedges known as *ikegaki* ('living curtains'), partly acting as wind-breaks but also, as is evident from the care with which they are shaped and trimmed, as decorative elements in the 'garden' landscape. Like the cypress in Italy, the poplar in France, or the eucalyptus in North Africa, the *sugi* (Japanese cypress) is used to mark the entrances to villages. Round the farmhouses bamboo frames run, carrying drying gourds or airing the night's *futon* (bedding).

PLATE 89: Paddy, Japan Sea coast

Although the main energies of farming communities go into rice, barley, wheat, tea—the edible crops that must be grown to feed the huge population from the very limited arable area—farms themselves often have small patches of bush- and flower-garden, and some areas are noted for their commercial cultivation of flowers: for example, the tulip fields of the Japan Sea coast, where paddies and luxury crops grow close to one another. Even here one is aware of the spine of rock and steep mountain behind, the enduring backbone of Japan, the source of so much of its beauty and its difficulty. From the mountains swift-flowing streams and rivers run, breaking into rapids and waterfalls, teeming with fish. They are steep un-weathered mountains because they are of comparatively recent geological origin, and have not yet been smoothed into the rounded shapes characteristic of English landscape; so the valleys tend to be both steep and narrow, and the plains are small and irregular. The whole feeling of the Japanese archipelago is of narrowness, constriction, and there are few broad horizons. Perhaps it is for this reason that Japanese art is intent on concentration—the limited, compact view, the microcosm of the *bonsai*, the single branch of peach-blossom, the tray-landscape. Seen in this way, perhaps the art of the Japanese sculptor is more faithfully represented in the carving of *netsuke* (small pieces of decorated ivory or wood, worn originally as purse-toggles and now collectors' pieces) than in the Daibutsu of Nara or Kamakura. 'Where man is not, nature is barren': in Japan, nature seems often almost a *product* of man, trimmed to his specifications, measured to his scale.

150

The craftsmanship of Japan is expressed in many skills. Wood, paper and clay are the traditional materials, and of all woods bamboo is the most celebrated and is used in countless ways—some more suitable than others. Fences, gates, poles, carts, the handles of tools and utensils, trays, furniture, the points of pens, the scaffolding of buildings, the implements of the tea-ceremony: all use bamboo, which is also a decorative motif found frequently in Japanese design, so that it has become something of a cliché.

But other woods are just as characteristically Japanese, from the pine to the *umoregi*, a fossil-wood found near Sendai and used for boxes and as display-stands for pottery and dolls. Wood is the basic material of houses, temples, boats, fans, and in the form of paper becomes screens, umbrellas, scrolls, and books. The basic Japanese toys are wooden, such as the *kokeshi*, a simple armless and legless doll made from two pieces of pine, the clothes and features painted in with strong, bright lines. And lacquer, a product of wood, has a history stretching back to the earliest period of contact with China.

Much hand-made paper is still produced, for example at Ogawa in Saitama Prefecture north of Tokyo. Here the mulberry bark is soaked in the wide shallow river, and the wet bark is trampled by women into a soft pulp: with further bleaching, drying and damping, it turns to the consistency of cotton wool, is treated with glutinous stuff, and then is peeled off as sheets of paper with the help of a bamboo frame. The result of this long and laborious process is sometimes paper for some fine book, but often the end-product is far more mundane—such as cheap hair-curlers. The texture of the paper used by modern wood-block artists such as Azechi and Ikeda is important, and is usually brought in to form an essential part of the composition.

But of all crafts, pottery is perhaps the one that the Japanese have brought to the highest pitch. Men such as Hamada and Kawai continue a tradition that has its roots in the primitive kilns still to be found all over Japan, and through the medium of Bernard Leach and other western potters the forms and glazes of Japanese pottery have influenced studio-potters everywhere in the world, who acknowledge Japan to be the leading country in ceramics. The potter's fidelity to material, simplicity of structure and receptivity to whatever *shibui* can give to his product, are continuing signs of an alertness and skill that, in other fields, has made Japan a country of truly modern craftsmen, in optics, precision engineering, and medical instruments. And the calligraphy of Japan—perhaps the craft on which it prides itself most—can be seen as clearly in many modern shop-signs as in the ancient screens and manuscripts. The fingers that hold a brush, make a paper lantern or a paper doll, and assemble a tiny transistor radio, are the same.

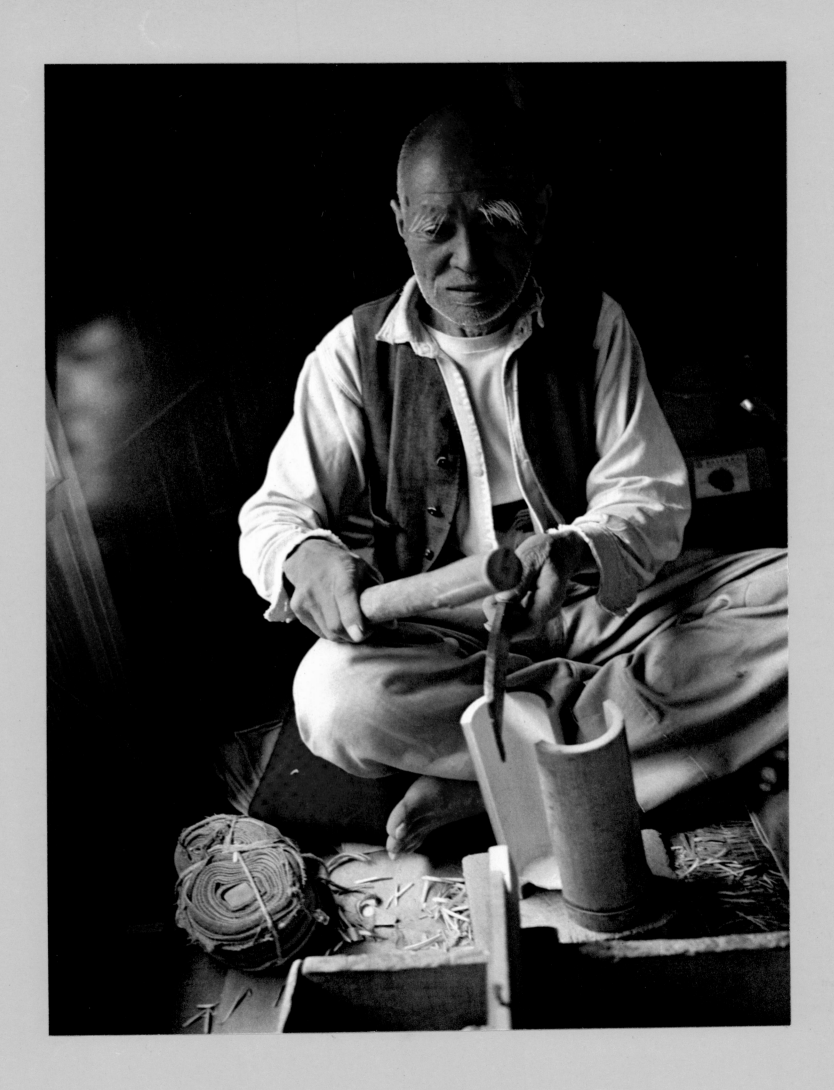

咲くからに
見るからに
花のちるからに
鬼貫

They bloom and then
We look and then they
Fall and then . . .

PLATE 92: Cherry trees, Gora, Hakone

The third and perhaps the finest of the 'Scenic Trio' is Matsushima, sixteen miles from Sendai on the north-east coast of Honshu. Matsushima needs no ancient precedent to reinforce its beauty. In a bay with a narrow entrance to the Pacific, hundreds of islands fan out as far as the eye can see. Well over two hundred of them have been named: Katsurashima (cinnamon island), Oshima (male island), and so on. Most of them are covered with pine trees, and Matsushima itself means 'pine island'. They are made of volcanic rock or of sandstone, full of labyrinthine caves, hollows and tunnels eroded by the sea and the wind. A few, such as Miyato, are inhabited, but most are so small that they support only the bent and precarious pines, though some of the uninhabited islands have temples or shrines. Close to the shore are several linked by bridges to the mainland and one to another. These slender, curved, vermilion bridges themselves form part of the composition, which is one of unity from multiplicity: dark green pines, white islands, blue sea.

These fragmented islands of Matsushima are like the product of some aboriginal act, some violent explosion of birth such as that which legend says resulted from the fusion of the ancient gods, Izanagi and Izanami, scattering the islands of Japan for 1300 miles from north to south. Matsushima is an image of peace, an ordered landscape, but behind it lies violence—of volcanoes, of weather, of men. Ruth Benedict used 'the chrysanthemum and the sword' to characterise the dual nature of Japan: the two are linked, as the dormant cherry and the dormant volcano are. The rising sun comes up over the Islands of the Rising Sun, of the sun-goddess Amaterasu, whose grandson descended from the plains of heaven to the mountains of Kyushu to reign over men. The legend has been obliterated, but it is still a powerful emblem of that primitive mystery which—beneath so many centuries of civilisation, so much sophistication and skill—lies at the heart of Japan.

156

PLATE 94: Mount Aso, Kyushu:
an active volcano

PLATE 95: Yasukuni Shrine, Tokyo:
dedicated to the war dead

Veiled in its smoke
The stone slumbers—
Mount Aso in spring.

Lifted for a moment,
Then dropping like rain—
The shrine's white curtain.

Index